Our
Christian
Republic
Assaulted

ISBN – 13: 978-1544684000

Title ID: 7008034

Second Edition

This book printed in the United States of America ——

J M Publishing Plus

2

Our
Christian
Republic
Assaulted

Our Republic has been assaulted from within, basically by the government we elected, the individual officals we chose.

George R. Melcher

Contents

Preface

I want to thank my Lord for granting me the strength and wisdom to articulate the ideas brought forward on these pages. Therefore the patience and fortitude with His enabling power, granting me an abundance of awareness and consideration to undertake such a very substantial project.

This book is a token of our Christian Republic and as such the consequence presents an image of the need for man's dependence upon God, without which he falters and fails. We began with an effective closeness and as the intervals past, we seek our dependences on individuals and a nation's government becomes paramount. After all these years one would think and come to terms with our bankrupt ideas and of failures, therefore by these means we have recklessly paved a path for disaster. Nevertheless God is there waiting to take our problems, unraveling them for us if we only let Him, as that is the nature of God and His love for we creatures which He has fashioned and created.

I have received much support from my partner over our many years together, I will not reveal how many. But will state my spelling is horrific and her help with this, for me remarkable. We ask God to bless our efforts. I hope these few words are realized and found helpful to rediscover our faith in God. Though some may find this a book on Christianity, rather a book of a Christian Republic's loss of their heritage, Christianity it's faith in God...

Introduction

The decision for writing this book was to describe the history of our Republic. Through an extraordinary and historic election of epic proportions, the year 2016. Thus by means of chronology, the description and clarification regarding our Republic's exciting history. Commencing and drawn from some seventy years previous to its triumphant conclusion in September of 1783. Then upon further examination, we found compelling support for a union between the colonies. I credit this as a result of the fortitude and resilience of the people who began assembling and began creation with the thirteen orginal sovereign colonies. Hence these men with Godly assistance worked out a Constitution of magnificent goals and attributes, rather small in size nevertheless a document of great significance, and unlike any other before or since.

While reinforcing the utmost assurance of God given unalienable rights, with a boundless Godly design, hence a practical freedom. This while the people of an envious observing world, with the ambiance and reorganization for the substance of freedom, it had never previously witnessed.

Therefore, one would expect the people to protect the inheritance given to us from God and the enormous sacrifice of the people who established our republic. Therefore we should expect progress and notable development in this new Republic, through fresh and many valuable viewpoints from the people and the Congress which they elected, with new plans and initiatives for developments of this young Republic nation.

Though more accurately in its place, we shall painfully discover an expression of first ignorance, lethargy and me first from the people and get all you are able, plus a nauseous government rearranging our Constitution or ignoring it completely, all elected by a comatose citizenry. This occurring throughout all of the three branches of a corrupt Republic, which has brought us to a new era, with the capacity for this devious attitude and magnitude of scope the founders definitely never anticipated, the Lincoln years.

Thus setting down of these words are my account and some clarification for the desire to present in the first portion, the era of pioneering. Therefore were successful through these years then noticeably concluded during the "Lincoln" war era and the evolutionary phase and chaos it brought to our young Christian Republic.

Consequently, amidst government corruption and the growth of an appropriation period, beginning the deteriorating years of our Christian Republic. Therefore, these historical events have chosen to stage the sanction and endorsement for failure. All due and expected for the failure to follow a God focused and inspired document, our Constitution. This in addition, was the institution crafted by man for an unscrupulous government, all designed for ignorant people and now headed toward a cataclysmic outcome.

As a result of these thoughtful words, Life, Liberty and the pursuit of happiness, many assume they are entitlements rather than God given experiences, plus an excellent opportunity for the pursuit of happiness. Originally and significantly intended for governments of the sovereign states, each would establish their own Constitution, laws and method they would exercise their faith in God. There were a few agreed upon rules put in place for a national government to fulfill and in addition appropriately controlled by citizens chosen from the sovereign states. Thus the national government was created, composed of people elected from and of whose power only existed and derived from the consent of those governed. Moreover this concept was so

innovative, unexperienced plus untested leaving most citizens
with a freedom never before established or in existence, however
entrusted for their undertaking.

This new liberty came adjacent to the time during which many
folks were moving west, as far as the Mississippi river and some
farther beyond.   While many people in the southern states
carried on farming quite successfully, advancing the agriculture
industry, with great cotton and tobacco plantations. Meanwhile
people in states to the north developed and improved upon
industrial concepts, plus new ideas for manufacturing which
advanced and improved production.

All the while fewer citizens engaged themselves in the national
government, or after time looked after their local government.
Therefore the National Government proceeded morphing our
Constitution and ideology into their own, slowly affecting and
changing power through merely awaiting and anticipating an
opportunity. Eager to exploit the prospect which whom those with
a lesser amount of awareness, those with the lack of knowledge to
the growing National government with its desire to arrest power
from each of the individual sovereign states.

Thus by 1850 there were 30 states with sixty Senators two
hundred thirty three House members. Their grotesque grasp for
power through continued proliferation of state sovereignty, still in
earnest until this very day. Let's not forget the reconstruction era
just prior to the turn of the century, was a disgraceful episode in
our history. After our humbled Republic went through a great
depression, World War Two, then another presidential
assassination, losing the war on poverty and Viet Nam, thus
creating these events literally assured our Republic the pathway to
socialism, largely seeking government's answer rather than God's.

This now requires we take a thoughtful examination into the situation we have arrived and are today confronting. While tolerating the most disgusting and repulsive liar ever to sit in the oval office. A man who chose claiming to be a Negro, rather than the Mulatto person he was born, again a lie, lying which began and became his mantra, notoriously deceiving our people. Then who became his closest ally, a socialist, Muslim woman named Valerie Jarrett. Why then should we be at all astonished concerning this year's election, two candidates both despicable persons. Again both being lifelong liars, cheats, and narsissist, one astoundingly evil. When their activities were exposed and their objectives revealed the people failed to revolt and such should have been undistinguished. As for Obama's future being sustained, still seeking ways to create chaos for our Republic. Then why should we be amazed or upset that we have been given this choice, when that of the so called elitist and informed people, have placed into position for the Presidency, either of two despicable individuals.

This now demands that we take a serious look at the situation we have created, along with the most disgusting and revolting cheat, while the majority accepts her as the utmost, obvious liar ever to compete for the office of the presidency. As she lied concerning Benghazi and the death of four men at the American Consulate, also effected unacceptable double billing customers at the Rose law firm, involved in the White Water real estate case. A woman who chose to claim and remained persistent of her innocence all the while the FBI had been investigating her use of her own server and misuse of government emails, practiced extreme negligence with secret documents and scandals, one could go on and on, as this is her record. An account of her entire life since college days, when her idol and a student of Saul Alinsky, a part of the Al Capone mob and author of Rules for Revolution.

Then we have another liar, cheat and thief, Donald Trump also a narcissistic individual who is tops at blasphemy, stating "he had no reason to ask forgiveness from God, God was a busy man and he had no necessity of Him". Vulgar language and blasphemy along with bashing other people was his reputation, he believes that he's a tough guy, only he's a sneak thief and coward, again one could go on and on but why, he's a despicable person, merely a blabbering buffoon.

Therefore within this book you will generally find a well-defined explanation of the facts and a few of my views on these issues, plus an analysis and suggestions for a healthier prospect of the future. I'm sure there is a person or persons, who have another proposal for the restoration of our Christian Republic's orginal goals.

The objective and desire for this book of our Christian Republic's history, was written for the reader to discover various examples, of our National government acquisition of power, once acquired, will then afterwards attempt to destroy our Republic.

While I have not an overall index, a description, justification and resource each of the words I placed together, each paving the way towards better consideration. I consider a current explanation of my facts and opinions are better shown for the period of and within each issue, rather an index at the end of this book. These are my explanations for doing so in this manner, data, information, facts and records at your fingertips.

Therefore, beginning with the first section which concerns early 1700's, we will quickly speak to the British control over the thirteen colonies and the Monarchs which ruled them. This early American history you probably remember from school days, but I will rush through them again. Then our Revolution and subsequent writing of the United States Constitution. A considerable look at the short Lincoln era and its consequences, the reconstruction period and on to the presidents thereafter. Thus exercising their use most clear, with familiar words to express each particular period, therefore many words considered to catch a glimpse of that period. Thus using the Constitution, actual events from history, statements from presidents and other relevant individuals, as you may come to reflect upon. Accompanying are verifiable records, documents, many laws and current articles. I hope these facts, ideas and opinions are complete enough to bring together and into view our Republic's past history and deep faith in God, which helps support my extensive and meticulous work with inclusive views. Hopefully these thoughts will have a significant effect upon the reader, give reason for greater participation and interest in returning to our Christianity and its' ideals, in spirit and in principle. There exists no other path or source to rely upon, only God and his son Jesus Christ.

Chapter One

The antithesis of our Republic's initial ideals, which led to its eventual downfall, but looking to rise once again.

The intended stance for this chapter is designed to express history as it's existed, thus viewed through facts, some of which are statements used for illustrations others may be unfamiliar to many. All of which are regarding our Republic's history and are in chronological order. I have chosen to write these sequences of historical events, actually as a report. Instead you will discover there are various distinct parts to this dissertation, spanning roughly 320 years. There are some facts that may not have been taught in grade school, or communicated at any level. Therefore preparing for this task by the selection and exploration of our Constitution and searching for truths beyond tentative history books. Facts must not be convoluted or weakened by those persons choosing dishonesty, offering only duplicity in the interest of an agenda for calculating organizations, which also incorporates political affairs. However alterations are not needed when conditions of an era prove to be essentially true to the event, thus honest and an impartial course will have been established. This matter is of course seen through your eyes, I ask no more than your honest participation in the consideration of the facts presented.

Secondly, an illustration of just how our current corrupt government, at its highest level has deprived or should I say, robbed the people of their autonomy. All the while devastating the core of our nation the middle class, the working people who are without a doubt, the one indeed stable portion of our Republic.

I have chosen the United States Supreme Court as a convincing example, revealing just how significantly politics has fallen to money, power and desire for self-worshiping, by way of bringing corruption into the public realm and to our Christian Republic's existence assaulted.

Then thirdly I question, where is our verve, our enthusiasm now? Why are we not once again conducting ourselves as our founders, developing our society, seeking help from our God? I believe there's an immense necessity for putting an end to these socialistic society and polices now. This failed theory (socialism) has existed knowingly, disabling the present government we ourselves have assembled and absolutely pursued as a society. We must rebuke and admonish those who have deliberately scorned God. In so acting disparage Christianity, plus committing crimes against our Republic and therefore its Christian ideals.

I think we are at these cross roads, the tipping point for the survival of our Republic, let me now quote the words of patriot Patrick Henry, *"Gentlemen may cry peace, peace, but there is no peace. The war is actually begun! The next gale that sweeps the north will bring to our ears the clash of resounding arms! Our brethren are already in the field. I know not what course others may take; but as for me, give me liberty, or give me death!"*
These words may sound stark or sharp, but it appears to me we have arrived at that position, the sound of clashing arms are nearing us and we have military all over the middle-east, I ask, on what course shall we wittingly and willingly proceed? It seems a catalogue of choices are not available, a decision by necessity is upon us and needs to be made at this moment. Nor will waiting until some later time be our choice, nor will the appearance of action, such as that taken by President Obama, a weak cowardly person. Only the dedication for reaching a winning strategy need be grasped, our goal has been chosen and scheduled for us.

Returning to the policy and intent of this book though conceivably undersized in volume, nevertheless written to reach the citizens of our once great Christian Republic, who in my opinion are gullible or generally unaware of why or how our union was formed by Christians exercising Christian concepts. Without question, unequivocally created the most brilliantly established form of governing administrated by man, however was originally initiated by God through wise men, then completed by men sacrificing their lives, fortunes and imparting their sacred honor.

While time or place is not paramount for reference for these actual events, however the early 1700 hundreds is a suitable and the largest part a substantial place to begin these painstaking introspective times. Thus this remarkable experiment called independence with personal liberty and owing only to God for those liberties given by Him, inaugurated initiatives and attitudes born of people with different objectives. All coming together from the thirteen colonies, each were quite determined this would materialize, if the people who governed people, by those chosen from the people and gathering their power from the consent of those governed, were instilled into each colony, while each colony persisted with their sovereign entities and with this ideology could become successful, so it became, and still the Constitution prevails.

The foremost consideration was sovereignty for each new state and each person therein and not controlled from far off England. I feel at this juncture with all good conscience, one only needs to suggest, now it's far off Washington D. C. today, which I believe is truly very far off, totality void of anyone or thing outside of the so called beltway, I believe we need a tightening of that belt.

Moving on, we find not all colonist felt that desire and with that their ideas were of different opinions. Such as protection from an invasion of France or Spain, this was their priority. This is where policy and political ideas clash. Therefore when exposing the launching for some of mankind's ideas, reactions to new and distinctively diverse ideas, generally create distinct and unexpected results, in the actions of others. Therefore a confrontation between the two ideologies ensued for about seventy years, including scores of individuals choosing a return to England.

However the story of those 13 colonies should begin with some descriptive goals and motivations. Therefore, first we will look at the Queen Anne era, as Queen Anne was the creature of several wars where land was either ceded to England by France or with an outright takeover, as was Nova Scotia, though however now a part of Canada. This following the William and Mary British rule of the American Colonies, however should be known for other than the so called "Queen's War", as the citizens were for the most part, without any or at least little, of the interest in any separation from England, generally considered their mother land. They found more freedom in colonial America and more business obtainability, thus exports all of their own making, though taxed accordingly.

Though originally named the *Concord*, it was a 200 ton merchant vessel built in England about 1710, was captured by the French one year later. Then transformed it, thus was modified to hold more cargo, including slaves, and renamed *La Concorde de Nantes*. Sailing as a slave ship, she was captured by the pirate Captain Benjamin Horngold a citizen of the city now known as Nassau in the Bahamas. Then 1717, near the island of Martinique. Hornigold turned her over to one of his men, Edward Teach (later known as Blackbeard), and made him her captain. Blackbeard then made *La Concorde de Nantes* into his flagship, adding cannon and renaming her *Queen Anne's Revenge*.

The account of Queen Anne's battle with piracy, especially Black Beard in particular is interesting. He and other pirates plagued shipping lanes off North America, and became a notorious English pirate who was active in the Caribbean and coast of North America from 1716 to 1718. He was particularly fearsome in battle. He made a deal with the governor of North Carolina in 1718 and for a time operated out of the many inlets and bays of the Carolina coast. Locals soon tired of his activities and an expedition was launched by the colonies. However the Governor of Virginia caught up with him in Ocracoke Inlet. Then a furious battle with Blackbeard and his men ensued, thus Blackbeard was killed on Nov. 22, 1718.

A bit more on Queen Anne known as the **Queen Anne style.** In Britain it refers to either the English Baroque architectural style, approximately of the reign of Queen Anne or of a revived form that was popular in the last quarter of the 19th century and the early decades of the 20th century in our country. All these factors were well accepted by the colonies.

Therefore little else has little if any importance to our analysis of this period of our Republic's History. Other than costume (dress) history information consists in this chapter in the first decade of the early18th dress in the 12 year reign era of Queen Anne 1702-1714 and taken from English Costumes by Dion Clayton Colthorp. The only other significnce in the life of Queen Anne was the County in which she was included. The Chesapeake Bay Bridge connects Queen Anne's of the Eastern Shore to Anne Arundel County on the Western Shore. Today the County has Diagnostics center locations throughout Anne Arundel County and has services available at each location and twelve different imaging procedures.

The next period for control of the colonies came from King George the First, who held a little tighter jurisdiction over the British Colonies. This brought some concern to a number of particularly politically minded persons.

However his rule ended 1727, while there was judiciousness in general, though some specific anxieties prevailed. Nonetheless begot and controlled calm, thusly predominated in the thirteen colonies. George the First, ruled as Great Britain's first

Hanoverian king from 1714 to 1727. He ensured a Protestant succession to the throne, but was not popular. A protest of any kind was not widely held, as the Protestant ideology were of several Denominations of Christianity that separated them from the Roman Catholic Church. Therefore based on theological or political differences during the Reformation were perceived as objectionable.

King George First was born on May 28, 1660, of Osnabruck Hanover Germany, to the elector of Hanover. He succeeded his father in 1697. When his mother, the granddaughter of King James I of England died, and he inherited the throne. He was part of the Whig Party, which was not popular in England. He forged an alliance with France, but narrowly escaped disgrace for questionable investments. He died of a stroke in the year 1727.

Nevertheless, King George the First era was interested and focused on two issues: one the European balance of powers, secondly the colonists' appropriation of land from the Native Americans. Although rivalry in Europe, between the French and British in particular, often influenced the course of events in their North American colonies.

Now George the Second was active in British foreign policy in the early years of his reign, was the son of King George the First. His shrewd diplomatic judgment enabled him to help forge an anti-Spanish alliance with France in 1717 - 1718.

In 1720 the South Sea Company, with heavy government and royal and aristocratic investment, collapsed. The resulting economic crisis made the king and his ministers extremely unpopular. Robert Walpole was left as the most important figure in the administration and in April 1721 was appointed first lord of the Treasury and in effect, 'prime minister'. His ascendancy coincided with the decline of the political power of the monarchy and King George indulged a lesser amount of his time involved in the British government.

King George II remained unpopular in England throughout his life, partly because of his inability to speak English but also because of the perceived greed of his mistresses and rumours concerning his treatment of his wife.

As effort increased by both the British and the French in order of their obsession, as the second king to rule England was more aggressive and began his rule in 1727 through 1760, it was by the progression of English Providence, the son of King George First, became the second Hanoverian to rule England.

Prior to his ascending the throne, King George First was faced with a rebellion by the Jacobite's, supporters of the Catholic James Stuart, who had a strong claim to the throne. This was concentrated mainly in Scotland, and was suppressed by the end of the year. Another smaller rebellion in 1719 was not a serious threat. The following year King George was again faced with a second rebellion by the Jacobite's and this was merely a token of resistance.

Meanwhile, at this time there arose a disturbing and disquiet existence and many colonist began to feel bitter about his attitude toward the colonies. He expended exploitations of the people, with new edicts while he was governing them. While thirteen colonies subsisted under British control, there was only moderate discontent, though this was not so easily accepted.

Provided through political and economic power, he consequently was able to maintain and strengthen both the British and French, as both were vying to acquire the larger share of the available land and maintain control over the new trading opportunities these colonies were providing. However during this period of time, the

European colonial governments tried to find ways to coexist with the original inhabitants, often by building alliances with certain tribes while triggering alienation with others. In spite of this, every so often as in the case of the French and Indian War, though known in Europe as the (Seven Year War). As a result in the European balance of power and politics, this situation had some consequences, as their activities merely resulted in bringing conflict within the colonies. As wars in Europe became more heated, fighting broke out between the French and the British in the American colonies. While both sides called upon Native American allies to assist them, exacerbating tensions between the tribes. Ultimately, the British Government found it necessary to pour additional troops and resources into protecting its possessions in the Americas and taxed their colonists to pay for these resources. These taxes eventually developed into a rallying cry and a colonist movement for their independence. This, plus a strong desire to exercise their faith as they believe it as such.

In England, all through his entire life his inability to keep the British constituents somewhat happy but also because of the growing passion by the populace in the colonies respectively more so in the American colonies.

In the meantime however, from the beginning of the eighteenth century, the demand for greater labor began, especially in the south where grain, cotton and tobacco happened to be their main commercial industry. Thus their commerce demanded greater amount of workers, thus the slave trade increased in a significant way. Although slavery actually began some one hundred years earlier, now at the earlier part of the 1700s the demand for slaves grew in an exponential manner for the need of more farm workers. They were White and they were slaves, also the name of an illumining book on this subject, written by author Michael Hoffman, a shock and unknown fact for most Americans today and I'm sure more so for Blacks than Whites . Brace yourself, as facts have become more remote or are unfamiliar to the majority of Americans, as those today have been exposed.

This was the result of awkwardness, for the most part we were never taught the true history of our Republic, there's more to come. As I've found *"telling the truth has become and appears to be a revolutionary concept"*.

The convicts and criminals; who were highly preferred by plantation owners, for the reason they were bound for 14 years. The child servants were praised for the same reason, a long period of bondage, Maryland and Virginia were convict states, receiving the Irish war prisoners and the Scottish Colossal Rebels. This along with the massive "Irish slave trade" all hidden from most our history books but it's the reality of our past history. Concerning this circumstance, it is written many times, in many books such as "White Cargo", "White slaves in Colonial America" and many more, found in your local library, or you may obtain them on amazon.com. On the whole slaves for the most of the eighteenth century were white, many by indenture servitude others outright slavery, little difference as indenture is a cutting on a contract, any contract written to the same objective on two separate pieces of paper with an angular cut, therefore, no alterations could possibly take place.

However when the purchaser of the individual person of servitude was confirmed, the purchaser kept both copies. Then let's not forget the Irish slaves, as it was they who presented a goodly portion of the slavery, not only in the colonies but elsewhere.

I find little if any difference between servitude and slavery, I've examined both Noah and Daniel Webster and found as stated primarily in the colonies, though elsewhere. Although these persons were not under servitude but slavery from English prisons.

It wasn't until the last portion of the 1700s, Africans became the inordinate number of slaves in the colonies under a few different circumstances. That matter is left to another book, another time.

Thus King George the Second, the only son of King George the first, born May 28, 1660, Osnabrück, Hanover [Germany] Died: 25-Oct-1760, location of death: London, England, and his Cause of death a stroke. Therefore his Remains Buried in Westminster Abbey, London, England.

The years which followed settled conclusively, at least for this reign, the constitutional question of the power of appointing ministers. The war between Spain and England had broken out in 1739. In 1741 the death of the emperor Charles VI brought on the war of the Austrian succession. The position of George II as a Hanoverian prince drew him to the side of Maria Theresa through jealousy of the rising Prussian monarchy. Jealousy of France led England in the same direction, and in 1741 a subsidy of £300,000 was voted to Maria Theresa. The king himself went to Germany and attempted to carry on the war according to his own notions.

Those notions led him to regard the safety of Hanover as of far more importance than the wishes of England. Finding that a French army was about to march upon his German states, he colluded with France gaining a treaty of neutrality for a year without consulting a single English minister. In England the news was received with feelings of disgust. The expenditure of English money and troops was to be thrown uselessly away as soon as it appeared that Hanover was not in the slightest danger. In 1742 Walpol was no longer in office. Lord Wilmington, the nominal head of the ministry, was a mere cipher. The ablest and most energetic of his colleagues, Lord Carteret (afterwards Granville), attached himself especially to the king, and sought to maintain himself in power by his special favour and by brilliant achievements in diplomacy.

George II, King of Great Britain and Ireland, the only son of King George I, was born in 1683. In 1705 he married Wilhelmina Caroline of Anspach. In 1706 he was created Earl of Cambridge. In 1708 he fought bravely at Oudenarde. At his father's accession to the English throne he was thirty-one years of age. He was already on bad terms with his father. The position of an heir-apparent is in no case an easy one to fill with dignity, and the ill-treatment of the prince's mother and by his father was not likely to strengthen in him a reverence for paternal authority. It was most unwillingly that, on his first journey to Hanover in 1716, George I appointed the Prince of Wales guardian of the realm during his absence. In 1717 the existing ill-feeling ripened into an open breach. At the baptism of one of his children, the prince selected one godfather when the King persisted in selecting another. The young man spoke angrily, was ordered into arrest, and was subsequently commanded to leave St. James's and to be excluded from all court ceremonies. The prince took up his residence at Leicester House, and did everything in his power to support the opposition against his father's ministers.

He had indeed done his best to exclude Pitt from office. He disliked him on account of his opposition in former years to the sacrifices demanded by the Hanoverian connection. When in 1756 Pitt became secretary of state in the Devonshire administration, the king bore the yoke with difficulty. Early in the next year he complained of Pitt's long speeches as being above his comprehension, and on April 5, 1757, he dismissed him, only to take him back shortly after, when Pitt, coalescing with Newcastle, became master of the situation. Before Pitt's dismissal King George II had for once an opportunity of placing himself in the populous of the country where they chose to be directed. To this end he had contributed much by his disregard of English opinion in 1743; but it may fairly be added that, but for his readiness to give way to irresistible adversaries, the struggle might have been far more bitter and had he separated from their side, though, as was the case of his grandson George III during the American Revolutionary war, it was then the popular side happened to be in the wrong. In the true spirit of a hard-liner, he wished to see Admiral Byng executed. Pitt urged the wish of the House of Commons to have him pardoned. "Sir", replied the king, "you have taught me to look for the sense of my subjects in another place than in the House of Commons." When King George II died in 1760, he left behind him a settled understanding that the monarchy was one of the least of the forces for which the policy had existed.

After some of the previous pages you have read, none of the events were lost to the colonist back in the New World crosswise to Europe, primarily Great Britain and France. The news coming from England to the shores of the colonies was not falling on deaf ears, as taxes grew so did their thoughts of freedom from the growing oppression, due to King George II and his aggression towards the colonies. In addition more and more of the colonist developed a need for some kind of intervention with the English Governors involved and grasping control of their lives. Others went so far as, thinking of something of an organized rebellious nature. Even war became a possibility, a thought felt as a result of a more aggressive mindset by a few individuals and their loss of freedom. Leaders of the colonist freedom movement wanted peace with England without direct confrontation, rather more control for the governing of their day to day life and the management of their future.

After all this and much more finally led to his death by stroke in Oct. of 1760. Hence came King George the Third. George III was king of Great Britain and Ireland from 1760 to 1811. The third monarch from the House of Hanover, King George III was just twenty-two years old when he succeeded his grandfather. Here we find a young man when he succeeded his grandfather. As king in 1760 his reign was shaped by the Seven Years' War (1756–1763), the Irish Rebellion (1798), and the French Revolution (1783–1815). However he is best known as the "tyrant", called by many as "unfit to become the leader of what was considered free people" Rather best known for his defeat after the Declaration of Independence July 4 (1776), the arrogant King who lost the American Revolutionary war (1776–1783). In reality, George III supported his cabinet's authority and, with a few exceptions, influenced but did not dictate policy; once the fighting began, he counseled his ministers to be consistent in their opposition to the American rebellion until his defeat at Yorktown. American patriots, hostile to British contemporaries, and nineteenth-century historians all painted George III as personally responsible for the conflict and its loss, but historical scholarship since the 1930s have reversed this anachronistic idea thus overly personalized their reading of the King. He had been stricken with poor health and a mental problem as King of Great Britain and the third monarch from the House of Hanover, remember George III was just twenty-two years of age at that time.

George III was born on June 4, 1738. His mother was Augusta of Saxe-Gotha (1719-1772) and his father was the Crown-Prince Frederick (1707-1751), who was known as "Poor Fred", because both his parents hated him. His father, George II, called Frederick *"the greatest villain that ever was born"*, his mother, Caroline of Ansbach, called him *"the greatest ass, and the greatest beast in the whole world"* and his sister Caroline (1713-1757) wished that *"he died and that we will all go about with smiling faces and glad hearts"*. Nevertheless, Frederick was a much better father to George than his father had been for him. He loved music and encouraged his children to appreciate it. He engaged reasonably competent tutors for his sons and they were taught Latin, French, and German history, along with mathematics and religion. The tutors found George a difficult pupil, not exactly unwilling, but *lethargic and incapable of concentration.* At times he was silent and morose and when he was angry, he became obstinate and sullen. At twenty he still wrote like a child.

Despite his loss to the American Colonist, George III was popular among his subjects in the decades following the war, and that fifteen years of his reign was totally celebrated countrywide in 1809–1810. In 1810, an attack of an illness, probably porphyria, which had plagued him for nearly two decades, robbed him of his sight, hearing, and sanity. On February 5, 1811, his son George, Prince of Wales, was appointed regent and ruled in his place until January 29, 1820, when George III died at Windsor Castle.

Consequently we return to the late-1700 and the assembling of our Constitution and the noble men who fought, struggled and died for the new republic. All but one colony that being Rhode Island, had signed the Articles of the Constitution in 1787. Nevertheless Rhode Island followed. Rhode Island became the 13th state to enter the Union after ratifying the Constitution. Ironically, the new state's late arrival came after the new federal government commenced on April 1, 1789, and the First Congress (1789–1791) had already passed 12 proposed amendments to the Constitution. Rhode Island was the only state not to send a representative to the Constitutional Convention. Only nine states were required to ratify the Constitution, and on June 21, 1788, the Constitution became the official governing document of the United States when New Hampshire ratified it. The "Hope State" made 11 attempts to hold a constitutional ratifying convention and held unsuccessful state referendums. The first referendum rejected the Constitution by ten to one. At great length, Rhode Island finally approved the

Constitution with provisional amendments. On August 31, 1790, the state's lone Representative.

It is my opinion each state had great distress, disquiet and fear of a national government. They in no way considered any loss to their sovereignty or to any entity, as they had started and finished a war to gain their autonomy. This was both a personal and state matter, each had their own Constitution first and foremost, with laws, rules and Christian ideals of their own.

Prior to the "Albany Plan of Union", was a plan to place the British North American colonies under a more centralized government. On July 10, 1754, representatives from seven of the British North American colonies adopted the plan.

Although it was never carried out, the Albany Plan existed as the first important proposal conceived by the colonies as a collective whole, united under one government, this notion ensued at the *Albany Congress.* Subsequently this plan became the united front by a Grand Council, administering a common policy for defence, and expansion, including that of the incorporation of Indian affairs.

Nonetheless the plan was thwarted by colonial legislatures and King George Second faltering. However, in reality it was an early indication that the British colonies were headed towards unification and a discreet interchange concerning a separation from Great Britain.

Prior to the notion with an idea regarding the "Albany Congress", a number of intellectuals and government officials had articulated and published several tentative plans for centralizing the colonial governments. Meanwhile Imperial officials contemplated the advantages of bringing the colonies under closer authority and supervision. Whereas colonists saw it as the need to organize and defend their common interests.

One figure of emerging prominence among this group of intellectuals, was fore mentioned Pennsylvanian Benjamin Franklin. As earlier, Franklin had written to friends and colleagues proposing a plan of "voluntary union for the colonies". On his way, the Pennsylvania government had already appointed Franklin as a commissioner to the Congress and upon his journey Franklin wrote to several New York commissioners, outlining brief hints towards a scheme for uniting the Northern Colonies thru measures enacted by the British Parliament.

The progression of events finally led the organization's ambitions for further and stronger agendas, guided by their own religious faith, rather than that of Great Britain's Anglican Church. This was to my mind, well on the path for God having originated His own intervention at this juncture.

It had long been understood that the prime motive for the founding of the New England colonies was religious freedom. Freedom for electing to worship God as they believed, this was a prime idea to living a faithfulness to God. Preferring what was a matter of their heart, thus what those early colonists wanted was the freedom to worship God as they deemed appropriate. Much of the religious disaffection, which a great topic had risen, and found its way across the Atlantic. This difficulty stemmed from disagreements within the Anglican Church, the Church of England, as it was known.

Those who sought to reform Anglican religious practices to "purify" the church became known as Puritans. They argued that the Church of England was following religious practices that had similarly and were too closely resembling Catholicism, both in structure and ceremony. The Anglican clergy was organized along these lines, with a hierarchy of bishops and archbishops. Puritans called for a Congregationalist structure in which each individual church would be largely self-governing. This concept by and large were adopted, therefore it was these actions and assessments thereof, which signified and was part of the beginning for the colonist revolt against Great Britain.

At this point it behooves me to stress this point, while though there were different protocols as how each church approached the way they worshiped God, it was the same God as there is only one true God and Jesus Christ His son. This you know as Christianity, the one in which many in our Revolution fought and died on behalf of.

The subject of their religious faith was only one of many connecting incidents, again a segment of the ultimate issues leading to the revolt aimed at their separation from European control, primarily England.

The Boston Tea Party in Dec. 1773 was significant, the American colonies undercut the business of colonial merchants. Prior to the Tea Act, colonial merchants purchased tea directly from British markets or smuggled from illegal arrangements. Then they shipped it back to the colonies for resale. Outraged by American merchants who undercut colonists initially in Philadelphia and New York, refused the tea from British East India Company, offloaded then sent the ships back to England. In many colonial ports to protest the Tea Act, the shipment of British East India Company tea was unloaded and then left untouched on the docks to rot, their repudiation of the Tea act.

The *Beaver*, *Dartmouth*, and *Eleanor* arrived in Boston in late November to the middle of December 1773. The colonists, led by the Sons of Liberty, wanted the ships to return to England, refusing the unloading of the ships' cargo of tea. Lieutenant Governor and Chief Justice of Massachusetts, Thomas Hutchinson, refused to let the ships return to England and held the Beaver, Dartmouth, and *Eleanor* in Boston Harbor until matters could be resolved and the tea offloaded. The framework for the Boston Tea Party was set, and on December 16, 1773, 340 chests of British East India Company tea were dumped into Boston Harbor accomplished by patriots, the Sons of Liberty.   After the Boston Tea Party the English Parliament responded in 1774 with many Coercive Acts, or as many seen it as the Intolerable Acts, which among other provisions, ended local self-government in Massachusetts closing Boston's commerce.

 Other colonists up and down the coast, thirteen Colonies in all responded in turn, the Coercive Acts with added acts of protest, and preceded into the convening, of the First Continental Congress, which petitioned the British Monarch (King George the third) for repeal of the acts.

This essentially organized the colonist and hardened the resistance to British control of their political and religious lives. Thus in consequence one might say in brief, the crisis escalated. Therefore the American Revolutionary War began from there, ironically near the city of Boston in April 1775 and the British capitulated on March of 1776.

   The next undertaking by the colonists was a total rebellion, after written three times on different occasions under a few slightly altered occurrences declaring and signing the Declaration of Independence, adopted by the Continental Congress on behalf of the thirteen colonies, on the **4th day of July 1776.** All Americans need remember this day, as it began the first day for individual freedom of life and liberty. Hence our Republic was born, coming about as the world's greatest form for governing, through the people, for the people, by the people. Oh how we have forgotten God and those remarkable new innovative set of tasks, with greater accountabilities. Today we act as though this idea has become out-of-date, we aren't up with the times, as a result anarchism and socialism.

As one could imagine the colonist outsized war began with England and would bring about their freedom from England and represent to all of Europe, a self-governing union of sovereign states, in essence a newborn Republic. Furthermore, these sovereign states would create a diminutive national Constitution with limited and enumerated powers, thus bringing together these sovereign states into a unification of efforts. Thereby establishing a Republican legislative body and occupied with full control by people from each state, chosen to represent each sovereign state individually, yet unified as enumerated in our Constitution.

Hence creating a republic of sovereign states, under God who had granted them freedom. Consequently bestowing upon them certain unalienable rights, among them Life, Liberty and the pursuit of happiness and to secure these rights, governments are instituted among men, deriving their just powers from the consent of the governed. The words and principles drawn from the Declaration of Independence.

This statement given at the Constitutional Convention by George Washington *"If, to please the people, yet we ourselves disapprove, how can we, afterwards defend our work? Let us raise a standard to which the wise and honest men can repair. This event is in the hand of God."* It seems quite obvious this new republic was formed and sustained by God and was shaped in Christian beliefs and principles, this throughout its laws, doctrines and values. Regardless of the many approaches of worshiping God, it was most certainly Christianity at the core of all practices of worship and the foundation of our united sovereign states.

Today as you walk up the steps to the building which houses the Supreme Court you can see near the top of the building a row of the world's great law givers and each one is facing the one in the middle who is facing forward with a full frontal view, what one's eyes will meet is Moses holding the Ten Commandments! Amen

James Madison, the fourth president, known as "The Father of Our Constitution" made the following statement *"We have staked the whole of all our political institutions upon the capacity of mankind for self-government, upon the capacity of each and all of us to govern ourselves, to control ourselves, to sustain ourselves according to the Ten Commandments given by of God."* Then we are obliged not to forget the man so intensely stated, "Give me liberty or give me death".

Patrick Henry, that patriot and another Founding Father of our country said, *"It cannot be emphasized too strongly or too often that this great nation was founded not by religionists but by Christians...not on religions but on the Gospel of Jesus Christ".*

Without any reservation or doubt this is a Christian nation, as in our pledge of allegiance today, "one nation under God" still remains in most of our schools. While that event along with the Ten Commandments have been removed from some courts, along with other public places doing so I say regretfully, without protest from Christians, WHY Thus appeasing particular groups who fail to understand our inheritance and what ought to guide our culture.

Our first five Presidents, George Washington was born Feb 22, 1732 - Dec 14, 1799 (age 67) an American politician and soldier who served as the first President of the United States from 1789 to 1797 and was one of the Founding Fathers of the United States. He served as Commander-in-Chief of the Continental Army during the American Revolutionary War and presided over the 1787 convention that drafted the United States Constitution. Life time marriage to his wife Martha. Then we have John Adam, who was born on Oct 30, 1735 - Jul 04, 1826 (age 90) a true American patriot who served as the second President of the United States and the first Vice President. He was a lawyer, diplomat, statesman, political theorist, and, as a Founding Father, a leader of the movement for American independence from Great Britain. He was also a dedicated to God and corresponding ideals, particularly with his wife Abigail. Third in the link of

Virginians came one Thomas Jefferson, Mr. Jefferson was an American Founding Father who was the principal author of the Declaration of Independence and later served as the third President of the United States from 1801 to 1809. Previously, he was elected the second Vice President of the new Republic he loved so much. Lost his wife to illness and was choleric with God over this situation. Our fourth to become President was James Madison, , (March 16 March 5, 1751 – June 28, 1836) he was an American statesman and Founding Father who served as the fourth President of the United States from 1809 to 1817. He is hailed as the "Father of the Constitution" for his pivotal role in drafting and promoting the United States Constitution and the Bill of Rights. Then we were honored with James Monroe, he was a share of the group that were the founders of this our Republic. James Monroe was an American statesman who served from 1817 to 1825 as the fifth President of the United States. Monroe was the last president resulting from among the Founding Fathers of the United States as well as the Virginian dynasty. He represented the end of the Republican Party in the presidency from that era, Born in Westmoreland County, Virginia.

The ideology of the founders persisted for another sixty five years, though a slight distancing did seem to begin after the tenure of these great and Godly men, beside others as Patrick Henry, Ben Franklin, and many others, too voluminous to observe at this time.

This ideology generally remained so until President Lincoln the tyrantical fool from Kentucky, who could find no support within the Constitution for his personal agenda regarding slavery nor was thie his true agenda, sovereignty of each state, this the core of his agenda was not in our Constitution. Thus quoting his words "god told him go to the Declaration of Independence" and found these words, "All men are created equal" consequently he proclaimed slaves were emancipated and the states were not sovereign. I ask, what should we find in his lonely and simple statement? "All men are created equal". How does it have anything what so ever to execute the idea, even a little, to work with the fact of the each state's own sovereignty? I am sure you will not find this ideology, or law in our Constitution, therefore the idea is completely unconstitutional. It is a fact, which he later stated, "in no way are Blacks equal to white people".

"Nevertheless, I find it ludicrous and preposterous, as it was obvious that slavery was truly never Lincoln's strategy or agenda, nor did he at this time have a coalition to support this way of thinking, sadly only a few northern businessmen who would profit from this choice of policies and never has the congress enacted it as law until 1968. The businessman were concerned that a tariff, import tax or export tax might apply, if the Confederates states were allowed to exist.

As a result his entire scheme was a fabrication, nothing more than stretching out the truth to fit his agenda, meant to destroy state sovereignty. In my thinking since Mr. Lincoln was assassinated, it would have been far more beneficial, had it been sooner than later.

Let us remember, 625, 000 individual souls died, do to this man and his tyrantical philosophy for governing our Republic. Thus in the following chapter we dig deeper into this individuals life.

Chapter Two

Lincoln, the wrathful man and his tyrantical policies

Time has brought us through our first fifteen presidents, from President George Washington by way of Presidents, Adams Jefferson, Madison, Monroe along with ten others till we come to President James Buchanan a two term president.

At this time there were numerous additional states (30), each having their own Constitution, laying down their own particular ideas concerning the law, rules on different subjects, and obviously opinions on slavery. As slavery was quite different in most of the states and diverse areas around the Republic. Consequently beginning in March 1857, the Supreme Court issued its decision in *Dred Scott v. Sanford case*; Chief Justice **Roger B. Taney** pronounced that blacks were not citizens, and derived no rights from the Constitution. Notice he never addressed the issue of white slaves born in the United States. I personally am not espousing or embracing a position, purely passing along the truth as it happened.

Regardless of the Supreme Court's decision, Lincoln's followers with his continued slogan "Lincoln's vision and theory", thus his idea concerning slavery and state sovereignty were pressing the length and breadth of the union. Why then should one bother to disquiet his butchery? We mustn't lose sight of his real agenda, ending state sovereignty, his forbidding a state to leave the Union, state autonomy existed since working with the ideas for the Constitution. In 1857–1858, Douglas broke with President James Buchanan, leading the fight for control of the Democratic Party. As a result and quite unexpectedly, Republicans even favored the reelection of Douglas for the Senate in 1858, since he had led the opposition to the "Lecompton idea of the Constitution", which would have admitted Kansas as a slave state. Therefore while in March 1857, the Supreme Court had issued its decision, in *Dred Scott v. Sanford*; of which Chief Justice Roger B. Taney presided.

Raised on the Mississippi frontier, was one Jefferson Davis, whose life was shaped by his brother Joseph, who was twenty-four years his senior. Joseph Davis made a fortune as a lawyer and planter, and he played a paternal role in Jefferson's life for many years. After Jefferson graduated from West Point and served in the army, Joseph gave him a plantation and the slaves to farm it. In the 1840s, Joseph managed the plantation so that Jefferson could go into politics.

Jefferson Davis became a staunch states' rights Democrat and champion of the unrestricted expansion of slavery into the territories. He was elected to the U.S. Congress in 1845, his only successful electoral campaign and then was appointed to the Senate after he became a hero while serving in the army during the Mexican War.

In the Senate he opposed the "Compromise of 1850", particularly the admission of California as a free state. This was a set of laws, which passed in the midst of fierce squabbling between these groups one favouring slavery and the other opposing it, thus an attempt to grant something for both sides. The compromise admitted California to the United States as a "free" (no slavery) state but allowed some newly acquired territories to decide on slavery for themselves. Part of the Compromise included the Fugitive Slave Act, which proved highly unpopular in the North. Senator Henry Clay was a strong force behind the passage of the compromise.

In 1851 he resigned from the Senate to run unsuccessfully for the Mississippi governorship. In 1853, President Franklin Pierce appointed Davis secretary of war. Davis served ably in this office and in 1857 re-entered the Senate, where he continued to advocate the spread of slavery into the territories. During the secession crisis, he resigned from the Senate and in 1861 was chosen by acclamation to become the Confederate President., thus a Confederate State was born. Meanwhile Abraham Lincoln was elected President of the Union, as the Republican Party was in desperate need of a candidate, thus Mr. Lincoln, became President Lincoln and was fighting against slavery, again stating which was obvious by then. Rather it was his gaining additional political support and much needed financial wherewithal. However in any event his true agenda was destroying state sovereignty.

As a result one would think he had a plan for the emancipated slaves, rather he failed to have any concern for the White slaves. I hope you haven't forgot the many white slaves as did President Lincoln. He was overcome, conceivably flabbergasted which caused a myriad of useless thoughts and ideas roaming his foggy anarchist mind.

All had little if any help, or entertained by congress, only his ludicrous ideas. As, send them back to Africa or to Puerto Rico, perhaps some other southern islands. It's this foolish man who brought about the deaths of 625,000 individuals for a proclamation which had no value. Rather in 1868 July 9th congress passed the 14th amendment stating "persons born or naturalized in the United States are citizens of the United States and in the state they were born". This was a far better solution than the one of President Lincoln which was advocated by himself. However as a matter of fact it never addressed the issue of state sovereignty, the need for his personal agenda, overpowered and subjugated the people, nevertheless 625,000 people died due to his selfish, fool hardy and mindless schemes. However this idea finally resulted in freedom for all slaves.

I presume one could possibly be capable of suggesting just how genuinely regretful this American civil war had become, over one man's lack of willingness to compromise with another, one Jefferson Davis. Jefferson Davis was correct due to the fact southern states wished only to exercise their sovereign right for withdrawal from the Union, forming a Confederate State. His statement and original idea came from the colonist when the U. S. Constitution was being drafted, as the colonies would never tolerate the thought of their sovereignty being taken from them.

In fact the thirteen colonies debated for more than three years to design our Constitution, of which state sovereignty was a foremost, prominently understood portion.

Lincoln followers denounced the Supreme Court's decision, alleging it was the product of a conspiracy of Democrats to support the slave power.- Lincoln argued, the authors of the Declaration of Independence never intended to say all were equal in color, size, intellect, otherwise moral developments, or social capacity', but they 'did consider all men created equal, equal for certain inalienable rights, among which were life, liberty, and the pursuit of happiness". Most slaves chose their lives, both white and black, some not so much the black, as countless were sold as goods.

Nevertheless, it was the will of the majority, hence were in agreement of joining together in union to better defend the sum total. An amalgamation of ideas to share with one another and of course industry needed a set rules for commerce, a market for export and to share ideas between each other. These concepts are for which they had been supportive, fought, died and intended from the very beginning, maintaining all were sovereign states, with their own constitutions, laws, rules even their own ideas for the concern over the divisions of Christianity.

President Lincoln failed to comprehend this idea and was not drawn to negotiations, or coexisting with a new State. Therefore, war was to him, his only alternative. The proclamation never mentions "all men are created equal", yet he said that was what some god suggested he would find in the Declaration of Independence as he failed finding support in the Constitution.

Significantly so, I later found where he stated it was "Constitutionally correct", yet I acquired or uncovered no such law, or in the least any suggestion of such an indication in our Constitution.

I have chosen to take the privilege of noting for all to read, President Lincoln's Proclamation, this is for your consumption and pondering, with your mind and heart, inclusive of the exponential threat posed to all states north and south. Ten years of reconstruction and generations of bitterness.

Thus his corrosive ideology: *Whereas, on the twenty second day of September, in the year of our Lord one thousand eight hundred and sixty two, a proclamation was issued by the President of the United States, containing, among other things, the following, to wit:*

"That on the first day of January, in the year of our Lord one thousand eight hundred and sixty-three, all persons held as slaves within any State or designated part of a State, the people whereof shall then be in rebellion against the United States, shall be then, thenceforward, and forever free; and the Executive Government of the United States, including the military and naval authority thereof, will recognize and maintain the freedom of such persons, and will do no act or acts to repress such persons, or any of them, in any efforts they may make for their actual freedom.

"That the Executive will, on the first day of January aforesaid, by proclamation, designate the States and parts of States, if any, in which the people thereof, respectively, shall then be in rebellion against the United States; and the fact that any State, or the people thereof, shall on that day be, in good faith, represented in the Congress of the United States by members chosen thereto at elections wherein a majority of the qualified voters of such State shall have participated, shall, in the absence of strong countervailing testimony, be deemed conclusive evidence that such State, and the people thereof, are not then in rebellion against the United States."

Now, therefore I, Abraham Lincoln, President of the United States, by virtue of the power in me vested as Commander-in-Chief, of the Army and Navy of the United States in time of actual armed rebellion against the authority and government of the United States, and as a fit and necessary war measure for suppressing said rebellion, do, on this first day of January, in the year of our Lord one thousand eight hundred and sixty three, and in accordance with my purpose so to do publicly proclaimed for the full period of one hundred days, from the day first above mentioned, order and designate as the States and parts of States wherein the people thereof respectively, are this day in rebellion against the United States, the following, to wit:

Arkansas, Texas, Louisiana, (except the Parishes of St. Bernard, Plaquemine's, Jefferson, St. Johns, St. Charles, St. James Ascension, Assumption, Terre Bonne, Lafourche, St. Mary, St. Martin, and Orleans, including the City of New Orleans) Mississippi, Alabama, Florida, Georgia, South-Carolina, North-Carolina, and Virginia, (except the fortyeight counties designated as West Virginia, and also the counties of Berkley, Accomack, Northampton, Elizabeth-City, York, Princess Ann, and Norfolk, including the cities of Norfolk and Portsmouth[)], and which excepted parts, are for the present, left precisely as if this proclamation were not issued.

And by virtue of the power, and for the purpose aforesaid, I do order and declare that all persons held as slaves within said designated States, and parts of States, are, and henceforward shall be free; and that the Executive government of the United States, including the military and naval authorities thereof, will recognize and maintain the freedom of said persons.

And I hereby enjoin upon the people so declared to be free to abstain from all violence, unless in necessary self-defence; and I recommend to them that, in all cases when allowed, they labor faithfully for reasonable wages.

And I further declare and make known, that such persons of suitable condition, will be received into the armed service of the United States to garrison forts, positions, stations, and other places, and to man vessels of all sorts in said service.

And upon this act, sincerely believed to be an act of justice, warranted by the Constitution, upon military necessity, I invoke the considerate judgment of mankind, and the gracious favour of Almighty God.

In my analysis of Lincoln's Proclamation, I discoved no plan for these thousands upon thousands of freed individuals. They were without food, housing, andf clothing and were told to go work, get paid and don't cause trouble. Of course the war still raged on, where were they to carry on and to what particular state. As the horrors raged on, their homes (for what they were) turn into ashes, merely burned and destroyed buildings by the army of the man who freed them, as previously stated, he was a fool without answers . This truly dire situation only grew, escalating everything and guilelessly turned more severe and ruthless, as at this point his own sense for some goal was unknown. The south was set ablaze, plundered, women raped and killed, children slaughtered. Need I continue with the gruesome details, as now coming methodically were his out of control incoherent, assumed military troops.

Again in President Lincoln's proclamation, one only finds retribution and reprisal for those demanding their right for going back to sovereignty of the individual states, moreover any state or part thereof, for failure to meet his demands. These demands for myself, sounded quite vindictive and tyrannical. Meanwhile let's not forget his Proclamations were for the Negro only, where was his much alarm and compelling expression for the significantly distressed White Slaves? There was none, as I had stated and will continue to reiterate it was about State sovereignty, which is why Abe Lincoln shall go down in history as saving the Union, from what? As the Union had little apprehension or anxiety roughly speaking, over the slavery issue. When in July 9th of 1868 the Fourteenth Amendment resolved that issue completely, and not a shot was fired.

If one takes notice, it is the first of countless moves on the part of the National government's seizing power, plus innumerable paths for affecting control of our Republic. Perhaps the people were merely apathetic, preoccupied simply with their survival than contending with the merciless, distorted and twisted national government, who lives with total disregard for the Constitution. I also suggest ignorance of the people, perhaps more interested with the local authorities and Christians merely wishing to get long, if that's true consider where we are today.

In hindsight, reflecting upon the chaos that ensued, the mirror image of all the damage the President's army inflicted, remains an observation for all to reflect upon. Perhaps a Reflection upon the view of rape, plunder, murdered women and children and burned fields, barns and homes. These words hopefully brings into sight the horrors effecting a revulsion in you. It was by far the cruellest, ominous picture of mankind, yes Lincoln led the most dreadful war executed by a tyrannical creature has ever put forward by this supposed human, happening within our Republic. Yet today this category of outrageous reasoning and ideology persist to reappear.

Remember the reconstruction era, another costly disaster by government, lasting ten years. The outcome, the south primarily coexisting by pressure, the south remained bitter, simply surviving for many generations. All this sorrow and anguish caused by one individuals' ego and desire for complete control with his need for totalitarianism, leading a tyrannical regime rather than a republican form of government.

After so much time spent on the Civil War and President Lincoln, despite the fact there are numerous books written on this subject, most but not all are in opposition to my numerous facts and few opinions on particular laws and dereliction of duty to the extreme intention.

This statement given at the Constitutional Convention by George Washington *"If, to please the people, yet we ourselves disapprove, how can we, afterwards defend our work? Let us raise a standard to which the wise and honest men can repair. This event is in the hand of God."* It seems quite obvious this new republic was formed and sustained by God and was shaped in Christian beliefs, principles and practices, thus throughout its laws, doctrines and values. Regardless of the many approaches of worshiping God, it was most certainly Christianity at the core of all practices of worship and the foundation of our united soveriegn states.

Again I wish to remind as we walk up the steps to that great building which houses the Supreme Court, we see near the top of the building a row of the world's great law givers and each one is facing the one in the middle who is facing forward full frontal view, one's eyes will meet Moses holding the tablet of the Ten Commandments!

James Madison, the fourth president, known as "The Father of Our Constitution" made the following statement *"We have staked the whole of all our political institutions upon the capacity of mankind for self-government, upon the capacity of each and all of us to govern ourselves, to control ourselves, to sustain ourselves according to the Ten Commandments given by and of God."*

Again I imagine it necessary to repeat myself. Patrick Henry, that patriot and another Founding Father of our Christian Republicsaid, *"It cannot be emphasized too strongly or too often that this great nation was founded not by religionists but by Christians...not on religions but on the Gospel of Jesus Christ"*.

Without any reservation or doubt this is a Christian nation, as in our pledge of allegiance to our Republic flag, "one nation under God" still remains in that pledge and remains in most, but not all of our schools. I in many places, official court grounds, public areas where a Monument to the Ten Commandments was recently over turned. This continually goes without protest from Christians who fail to comprehend our inheritance which ought to guide our culture. Where may I ask are the Christians whom are the required individuals whom fundamentally are the ones obligatory to protest such actions?

For a case in point, in my area I have spoken with Timothy Green pastor at the Cottonwood Christian Fellowship Church in Alamogordo New Mexico. This about the superior positioning of the American Flag and the Christian flag, which would fly the highest, I felt since it was in the wrong position on Highways U.S.70 &54, therefore many non-Christian would observe our opinion of our belief in Jesus Christ. However he was adamant the

American flag had prominence, this he said because of the phrase "one nation under God", and besides being incorrect I find his answer quite childlike. I then explained until the turn of the 20th century there was no pledge, and in addition till 1954 those words he spoke of, were non-existent. What happened, nothing, another cowardly or conceivably another poor example of Christianity, failing to denote the significance to the meaning of Christianity?

What is Christianity? I believe the words Christian or Christianity are words used to signify a faith based practice on the teachings of Jesus Christ, to such an extent embodied in the New Testament, emphasizing the protagonist of Jesus Christ as our Savior. Furthermore, God said he was the Alpha and Omega, the very Beginning and the End, stating he was a jealous God and to place no god before Him. (Read Genesis: 20,1-5). Then we were warned concerning the evil of governments. This in all my heart, I believe is what the Christian Flag embodies, every fraction of our faith, and God expects nothing less.

Discovering so, but I find it astounding, while less than a mere seventy five years, we the People succumb to a man (Lincoln) so inflicted with tyranical and considerable imbecilic schemes. One is stunned to find that he had been elected to the presidency, perhaps due to his corrupt ideology, plus along with the corrupt people he associated with earlier. Hence leading them/us to chaos, after which the people followed like sheep down a path of obvious lies. This man suspended the Writ of Habeas Corpus and jailed all who contradicted or dissented against him, including judges. Closure of the press if they felt obligated by their grasp of the truth, to print conflicting thoughts or struggled against his brutish and outrageous ideology.

Yet not a whimper was heard from so called Christians, they remained silent, the silence actually defining and old Abe marched on, leaving an inaudible path of death from 625,000 departed souls, left behind. Rather the landmark federal legislation which prohibited discrimination on the basis of race, color, religion, sex and national origin never arrived upon the scene until The Civil Rights Act of 1964. This granted equal entry to employment, schools and public spaces. Accordingly, yet Lincoln remained without strategies or arrangements for the emancipation of the Negro or any slaves from the rebellious states, after they had gained their freedom they were lost for one hundred years.

In the same fashion, he had failed to form any concepts or proposals from an operational viewpoint to solve this conundrum. All these free persons he had positioned into a society being utterly unprepared for such a situation. I ask where would they live, work or worship, it only grew more corrupt and ruthless. I am aware many books have been written turning him into a godlike creature, ultimately for myself I have seen no compelling reason to think likewise, or respect for their ideas.

As time marched onward the entire Republic remained in disarray, turmoil and disorder. It seemed again that Christians refused to call upon God for guidance were absent from realism as this misery grew and grew until the fore mention Civil Rights Act of nineteen sixty four, signed by a loudmouth from Texas, Linden B. Johnson .

Once again, more than fifty years later indications shows no negligible improvement between White and Black individual relationships, none what so ever. While the sixties were a reoccurrences of political crossed and signals to many. I find them occurrences of diverse issues and mean while the people chose poor leaders, unable to properly guide, or incapable to lead through these turbulent times. Acts such as those regarding the lack of governmental action, better stated inaction, imagining these confusing issues reminds you of events overwhelmingly affecting our Republic currently.

I have arrived at my personal conclusion, brought about through an analyzation and by some rationalization, there is but one solution to the serious enigma presented by the presence of the Negro person in our Republic. Regardless of all the political chatter there's one thing I am sure, and that inasmuch as the Negro is here and can neither be dispatched nor driven away, as they are at this juncture here to stay and rightfully so. Today and in the future remain a part of our Republic as from the beginning. The only wise and principled Christian objective continues without any change. It seems to me, which should occur is treating each individual without preference to any peculiar race, nothing more than strictly upon their qualities as a person. Therefore giving them no more and no less than they show themselves worthy and willing to produce, plus making some particular obligation to one another and too our society as a whole.

Conversely, all help from government needs to be reduced to a bare minimum, then if necessary by the particular states where they reside, as the particular state should know the problem and able to resolve the issue which, where and how they may occur.

I am firmly of the opinion it is the duty of the churches to help and support people in need, what's more the church is much closer to those needs and are by far the best acquainted with them. Therefore, best able to discern how to identify the need for assistance. Moreover, the local churches should have knowledge of employment in their area, having a greater ability to assist the distinctive abilities of individuals for the needs and the requirements of the employer. Earlier in our Republic's existence, there were no welfare programs being structured and operated by government, in particular the national. However I'm obliged to bring to mind the birth of our Republic and the basic need to return to the thinking of that period of time. Thus returning to our Republic's noble history, shifting to a little earlier era, perhaps a bit less transitory, therefore far greater solutions would come about.

I have chosen the application of presidents as a time period, therefore the chore of leading the policies and politics of our Republic's history. I have chosen presidents as my selection to separate one time and or era from another, as they are well recognized for their political ideology, some may be bombastic in their style. Nevertheless, we shall proceed, with as great a coverage as may be possible. However I wish to bring God and Christianity, once again front and center into this project, without whom there would be no necessary reason for it at all. Our founders seemed to desire Him quite essential to their plans and future. I see a far greater need for correspondence with Him for my choice of words, likewise a similar basic prerequisite for our Republic today.

In closing one more sketch of President Lincoln, in this man, I find him to have been wrathful and revengeful and foolish.

During the Civil War, President Lincoln implemented several questionable constitutional measures to preserve the Union. I am of the opinion he had no basic necessity to save the Union, if any reason was had the south become a free and separate country, goods purchased would have an import tax applied. The business men and their end products in the north existed primarily from goods and crops which came through the south. Most dramatically, he suspended the writ of habeas corpus on eight occasions, thus empowering military commanders to imprison thousands of civilians without any recourse to the courts. Moreover, some 300 allegedly disloyal newspapers were shut down, at least temporarily, this by military and civilian authorities, and mobs often attacked anti-administration presses for what was considered their disloyal expression.

The Swedish engineer John Ericsson was a ship designer and also he designed the USS *Monitor*, the ship that ensured Union naval supremacy during the American Civil War. A memorial to his involvement is just below the Lincoln memorial.

Let's remember his proclamation concerning the slaves and the revengeful attitude he exercised toward the southern states, makes Lincoln nothing but a common criminal. While assassination was not the answer needed, a trial would have therefore stood unambiguously exposed his vile and loathsome activities against our Republic and its people.

I am aware my words have subsisted steadfastly in bringing down the idea Lincoln (if that was his name, just another of his many controversies) as a hero an American protagonist.

Let's work together looking towards an accompanying, tangible and spiritual thinking on his complete authentications, this upon his many problematic public life circumstances.

Chapter Three

**My explanation for some of our Republic's history since the
end of the Civil War and the turn of the Century**

Now a man more strikingly by means of his many substantial
political manipulations, he astonishingly became our president
quite by accident, one day vice president next day president. This
of course involved President McKinley and his death in order for
this event to occur, placing Vice president Theodore Roosevelt into
the position of President of the United States of America.

This resulted in an American politician, author, Theodore
Roosevelt Jr. was explorer, soldier, naturalist, and reformer, he
served as the 26th President of the United States from 1901 to
1909. He also served as the 25th Vice President of the United
States and as the 33rd Governor of New York, plus leader of the
Republican Party.

During this time, he became a driving force for the Progressive
Era in the United States in the early 20th century. His face is
depicted on Mount Rushmore, alongside those of George
Washington, Thomas Jefferson, and others.

As stated up to that time he saw little worth in congress, thus he
set out to build the Panama Canal Zone, however the cost to
construct the Canal Zone was $375 million, including $10 million
paid to Panama plus $40 million paid to the French Canal
Company for the rights to build the canal. Moreover, the bodies
beyond that of 22,000 men, plus irritating the Columbian
government. Of course this was no problem as he brought in two
battleships, which ended the Columbian concerns!

With the assassination of President McKinley, Theodore Roosevelt, not quite 43, became the youngest President in the Nation's history. He brought new excitement and power to the Presidency, as he vigorously led Congress and the American public toward progressive reforms and a strong foreign policy.

His ideology was that the President as "a guardian of the people" should take whatever action necessary for the public good unless expressly forbidden by law or the Constitution." I did not usurp power," he wrote, "but I did greatly broaden the use of executive power."

Roosevelt's youth differed dramatically from that of Presidents like Lincoln. He was born in New York City in 1858 into a wealthy family, but he too struggled against ill health and in his pride became an avid supporter of the strenuous life.

In 1884 his first wife, Alice Lee Roosevelt, plus his mother died on the identical day. After which Roosevelt then spent much of his next two years on his ranch in the Badlands of Dakotas. There he overcame his sorrow as he lived in the saddle, driving cattle, hunting big game. On a visit to London, he married Edith Carow in December 1886.

During the Spanish-American War, Roosevelt was lieutenant colonel of the Rough Rider Regiment, which he led a charge up San Juan hill at the battle of San Juan. He was one of the most overblown heroes of the war.

Boss Tom Platt, needing a hero to draw attention away from scandals in New York State, accepted Roosevelt as the Republican candidate for Governor in 1898. Roosevelt won the election and served with his particularity difference as expected.

As President, Roosevelt held the ideal that the Government should be the great arbiter of the conflicting economic forces in the Nation, especially between capital and labor, guaranteeing justice to each and dispensing favors to none.

Roosevelt emerged spectacularly as a "trust buster" by forcing the dissolution of a great railroad combination in the Northwest. Other antitrust suits under the Sherman Act followed.

Roosevelt navigated the United States more aggressively into world politics. He enjoyed to quote a favorite proverb, "Speak softly and carry a big stick".

Aware of the strategic need for a shortcut between the Atlantic and Pacific, Roosevelt ensured the construction of the Panama Canal. His corollary to the Monroe Doctrine prevented the establishment of foreign bases in the Caribbean and arrogated the sole right of intervention in Latin America to the United States.

Teddy Roosevelt was a two term president, after a hunting hiatus he chose to try again for the Bull Moose Party. However, though he still had a yearning for politics, his manner, bombastic and impetuous style , caused his loss. However his suffer defeat, therefore ending what he assumed was his political life. There was surprisingly little else to say after a very amazing life and presidency, losing in his final attempt for the presidency. Returning to what he loved best, hunting and so he did in the state of Montana, dying in Jan. of 1919.

Reasonably we must visit William H. Taft U.S. president from 1909 to 1913 and chief justice of the U.S. Supreme Court from 1921 to 1930, William Howard Taft became the only man in history to hold the highest post in both the executive and judicial branches of the U.S. government. This man a predecessor of Teddy Roosevelt our all American hero.

Despite his pledge, Taft lacked Roosevelt's wide-range view of presidential power, as well as his charisma as a leader and his physical vigor. Though he was initially active in "trust-busting," initiating some 80 antitrust suits against large industrial combinations twice as many as Roosevelt. Thus he soon after backed away from these efforts, however in general aligned himself with the more conservative members of the Republican Party. In 1909, Taft's convention of a special session of Congress to debate tariff reform legislation spurred the Republican protectionist majority to action and led to passage of the "Payne-Aldrich Act", which resolved little in an effort for lowering tariffs.

Though more progressive Republicans (such as Roosevelt) expected Taft to veto this bill, surprisingly he signed it into law and publicly defended it as "the best tariff bill that the Republican Party ever passed."

In another key misstep where progressives were concerned, Taft upheld the policies of Secretary of the Interior Richard Ballinger, and dismissed Ballinger's leading critic, Gifford Pinchot, a conservationist and close friend of Roosevelt who served as head of the Bureau of Forestry. Richard Pinchot's dismissal split the Republican Party further and estranged Taft from Roosevelt for good.

Often overlooked in the record of Taft's presidency were his achievements, including his trust-busting efforts, his empowering of the Interstate Commerce Commission (ICC) to set railroad rates, and his support of constitutional amendments mandating a federal income tax and the direct election of senators by the people (as opposed to appointment by state legislatures).

Undoubtedly relieved to be leaving the White House, Taft took a position teaching constitutional law at Yale University Law

School. In 1921, President Warren Harding fulfilled Taft's lifelong dream by appointing him chief justice of the United States Supreme Court. In that post, Taft improved the organization and efficiency of the nation's highest court and helped secure passage of the Judge's Act of 1925, which gave the court greater discretion in choosing its cases. He wrote some 250 decisions, most reflecting his conservative ideology. Taft's most prominent opinion came in Myers v. United States (1926), which invalidated tenure of office acts limiting the president's authority to remove federal officials. Taft remained chief justice until shortly before his death, on March 8, 1930, from complications of heart disease.

The entry of the United States into the First World War in April 1917 we were an associate, not an ally of the Allies, was more than just a response to submarine warfare; it also reflected the vision of President Woodrow Wilson, who had been inaugurated as the 28th president of the United States.

Thomas Woodrow Wilson was an American socialist politician, an academic who served as the President of the United States from 1913 to 1921. A member of the Democratic Party.

President Wilsons's plan for the future seemed quite socialistic, he had outlined in the "Fourteen Points envisioned for restoration and a more stable organization of the "League of Nations", of which our Republic never joined based on a consensus of the great powers". Due in large part to Wilson's vision, the United States had changed course from isolation toward engagement.

In early January 1918, both British Prime Minister David Lloyd George and American president Woodrow Wilson issued public explanations of what they hoped to accomplish through a victory over the Central Powers. Wilson received input from his closest advisor, Colonel Edward House, and a number of academics, who were known as "The Inquiry." The resulting Fourteen Points were presented in a speech before both houses of Congress and were intended to generate support for Wilson's vision of the post war world, both at home and also among allies in Europe. Further, the president hoped that the promise of a just peace would be embraced by the populations in enemy nations and generate momentum for ending the war.

Allied governments paid lip service to the Fourteen Points while the fighting continued. Those nations needed American financial might to assist in their rebuilding after the war and did not want to risk offending Wilson. There was some fear in Europe the United States might seek a separate peace with Germany, freeing that nation to continue the fight without the presence of American forces.

In his speech to Congress, President Wilson declared the fourteen points which he regarded as the only possible basis of an enduring peace. They were, according to him a peace procedure, which that nation would not continue the fight without the presence of American forces. The United States would of course be leading, as a result of, and in my opinion a socialist approach to leadership, this would be his socialist peace leadership.

Wilson's 14 points were, five of the Fourteen Points dealt with issues of broad international concern. The next eight points referred to specific territorial questions. The last was an Association of Nations which the United States never joined. However it did appear to fall apart and so did his presidency.

As the 1920 U.S. presidential election approached, rank-and-file delegates to the Republican National Convention chose Coolidge as the vice presidential candidate on a ticket headed by U.S. Senator Warren G. Harding of Ohio.

The Harding-Coolidge ticket won in the election in a landslide and the men took office in March 1921. Then as life is unable to account, just two years later, Harding's death on August 2, 1923, unpredictably hurdled Coolidge into the Oval Office. He appointed a special counsel to investigate the Teapot Dome oil-lease scandal (in which the U.S. Secretary of the Interior was accused—and later convicted—of accepting bribes to lease federal oil reserves without competitive bidding), and he dismissed Harding's tarnished U.S. attorney general, Harry M. Daugherty. Coolidge's reputation for honesty and integrity helped him restore public faith in the national government.

Coolidge ran for president in 1924 and won decisively, the next election was dismissed by himself, as he stated he was tired and had served his country.

Herbert Hoover a Republican, became president of our declining Republic, taking office in 1929, the year that our U.S. economy plummeted into the Great Depression. Although his predecessors' policies undoubtedly contributed to the crisis, which lasted over a decade, Hoover bore much of the blame in the minds of the American people. As the Depression deepened, Hoover failed to recognize the severity of the situation or to leverage the power of the national government to squarely address it. A successful mining engineer before entering politics, the Iowa-born president was widely viewed as callous and insensitive toward the suffering of millions of desperate Americans.

After capably serving as Secretary of Commerce under Presidents Harding and Coolidge, Hoover became the Republican Presidential nominee in 1928. He said then: "We in America today are nearer to the final triumph over poverty than ever before in the history of any land." His election seemed to ensure prosperity. Yet within months the stock market crashed, and the Nation began a cork screw descent into an enormous depression.

After the crash Hoover announced that while he would keep the Federal budget balanced, he would cut taxes and expand public works spending. When the Wall Street Crash of 1929 struck less than eight months after he took office, Hoover tried to combat the ensuing Great Depression in the United States with large-scale government public works projects such as the Hoover Dam, and calls on industry to keep wages high. He reluctantly approved the Smoot–Hawley Tariff of 1930, which sent foreign trade spiralling down. He believed it was essential to balance the budget despite falling tax revenue, so he raised the tax rates. The economy kept falling, and the unemployment rate rose to 25%, while the heavy industries, mining, plus wheat and cotton farming were hit an especially hard blow. This downward spiral, plus his support for prohibition policies that had lost favour, set the stage for Hoover's overwhelming defeat in the 1932 elections

In 1931 repercussions from Europe deepened the crisis, even though the President presented to Congress a program asking for creation of the Reconstruction Finance Corporation to aid business, additional help for farmers facing mortgage foreclosures, banking reform, a loan to states for feeding the unemployed, expansion of public works, and drastic governmental economy.

At the same time he reiterated his view that while people must not suffer from hunger and cold, caring for them must be primarily a local and voluntary responsibility.

As a result, Hoover was thoroughly defeated in the next election, thus in 1932, the entrance of Democratic presidential candidate,

Franklin D. Roosevelt and his victorious results. He became the thirty-second president of the United States.

Again I 'm confident in assuming you have taken notice and realize I have chosen to point out the weaknesses, plus the character of presidents. My reason in so doing, is we have elected these men since they were supposed leaders thus capable of the task, that of befitting presidents. These men are probably most known for their achievements or lack thereof and many clearly known for voluminous words and their political conflicts. Thus their actions are beneficial and remembered by all citizens of the Republic.

Since the activities and words which were at best a goal are choicest and best to recollect for our citizens. Therefore, it is those persons I have selected, perhaps a bit offending or upsetting to some. Executing and sorting out my thoughts in this way to you the reader. If so I am a bit pained and apologetic, nevertheless it's my right and duty, however it's proper for me to answer for my so doing.

Chapter Four

This chapter covers the mid and last years of the twentieth century

Now life follows into what I actually believe are the true reasons for the breakdown of our once great Republic, the people's failures and disbelieve in God, the same God which so abundantly blessed us and who inspired the men who gave their lives so we could become the recipients of immeasurable freedoms and liberty of life, an unalienable right gifted and granted by God..

It is we Americans, who so inadequately treasure the wealth of these meaningful concepts and profound designs articulated in our Constitution, again inspired by God. Yet we have forgotten and neglected His love toward us, while still being communicated with and visited upon our fragile Republic. Fragile despite these facts, we continue onward, we persist to overlook and disregard His righteous presence in our nation.

A statement by Thomas Jefferson shows how despaired and again I remind how great his challenge became for the nation he loved, as an example, *"I tremble for my country when I reflect that God is just; that his justice cannot sleep forever"*. Those men, our presidents are merely a mirror image of we the people, I ask to whom is the responsibility and competency of bringing forth great leaders, it is the people. It may well have come about, precisely due to the considerable absence of God in our society and numerous deficiency in an abundance of arenas.

Reading this you probably assume I'm preaching, when honestly I am simply writing only the facts, as seen through the eyes of an individual well into his years and are given for your consideration and possible adaptation.

A man who has lived nearly a third of our Republic's history, beginning with its adoption of our Constitution in September of 1789 including the Bill of Rights in 1891. However I am accurate by saying there are many, yea, an abundance of persons whom definitely will not accept the thinking of any elderly man.

Therefore, let me present some statistics on the gross degeneration in America today, after stating I have observed and experienced much while researching and studying for the support of my analysis and assertions.

New Mexico my adopted home state, are performing abortions after the 20th week, highest in the nation. New Hampshire, where 30% of 18-25 year olds are using illegal drugs. Washington State nearly 20% of the people are atheist and the state of Oklahoma has the highest incarceration rate per capita in the Republic. In Florida every 5.6 minutes a violent crime is commited, Vermont 50% of people never go to church and in Idaho 2 in 3 say they have no active faith in Christ.

Furthermore, we find that all one is required for the execution of changing their gender, is merely saying what they believe their gender is, "whatever they proclaim", or what they should have develop into whatever it may be. I ask, how would that process work with the prison authorities? If I'm a man but say I'm a young girl am I sent to a female prison, or if I'm a woman but see myself as a man, am I allowed to join the men's nude swim club or by mentally switching, play football..

I shall continue, some 37 years after Roe v. Wade, **50 million babies have been killed** and yet the United States is still continuing to abort babies with no end in sight.

Another profound statistic, I have found that 51 percent of Americans agree with this statement: "I believe it is necessary to give up some civil liberties in order to make the country safe from terrorism." As if going through airport security was not enough of a hassle, now it's found TSA employees are incompetent, lazy individuals.

While writing this an individual at the Fort Lauderdale Fla. Airport a gunman wearing a "Star Wars" T-shirt opened fire at a baggage carousel on Friday, killing at least five people before being taken into custody by officials and witnesses said eight were wounded in the incident. It was reported Police shot the shooter as he attempted to reload, as MSNBC misreported, citing witnesses. Some witnesses said the man, who said nothing, appeared to be in his 20s. One person was injured trying to evacuate, which may have triggered the later panic, an Israeli witness said. Dozens of police sprinted back and forth with automatic weapons drawn, and one officer screamed "Get down, get down!" from a nearby parking garage, as witnessed by a Reuter's reporter.

Once more perhaps even closer at home, a depraved attack on a mentally disabled white teen broadcasted live on Facebook allegedly by four black Chicago-area residents became a national whisper. Thursday conservative pundits tried to pin the blame for the attack on the Black Lives Matter movement. Shown repeatedly on cable TV and shared tens of thousands of times online, the grotesque video of the 18-year old being cut with a knife to the scalp and forced to drink toilet water led familiar right-wing talking heads including Glenn Beck, Milwaukee County Sheriff David Clarke and others to call for increased charges and to stop finding fault with what some charged and characterized as excessively unrestrained policing. All this without a statement from President Obama, Al Sharpton or Jessie Jackson, beside other racist leaders. I ask, Is this all not part of the degeneration of our Republic?

Gladly moving on I will try and explain the abnormal statement by John Adams feebly *saying,* The United States government is not, in any sense, founded on the Christian religion. Subsequently it was *the Constitution* for the **United States** which was secular and not the citizens, rather they were as a whole Christians. The design was for Congress to *make no law respecting the establishment of religion, nor prohibiting the free* exercise *thereof,* found in the Bill of Rights, First Amendment section one, part of the Constitution. However, I believe Congress was chosen by a Christian electorate, during that time in the early years of our Republic.

George Washington *"I am sure there never was a people, who had more reason to acknowledge a Divine interposition in their affairs, than those of the United States, and I should be pained to believe, that they have forgotten that, which was so often manifested during our revolution, or that they failed to consider the omnipotence of God, who is alone able to protect them".*

Then there is one Patrick Henry: "This is all the needed by inheritance I give to my dear family. The religion of Christ will give them one which will make them rich indeed". Again we find these words quite inspiring...
"Is life so dear or peace so sweet as to be purchased at the price of chains and slavery? Forbid it, Almighty God! I know not what course others may take, but as for me, give me liberty, or give me death!" Where are those men today... *"Three million people, so armed in the holy cause of liberty, and in such a country as that which we possess, are invincible by any force which our enemy can send against us. Beside, sir, we shall not fight our battles alone. There is a just God who presides over the destinies of Nations, and who will raise up friends to fight our battles with us".* *"The Bible*

is worth all the other books which have ever been printed", Patrick Henry.

Returning to one John Adams we witness him in a different mode, one still about our government, Constitution and religion, except however in a new statement. *"The Constitution was made only for a moral and religious people. It is wholly inadequate to the government of any other".*

"Only virtuous people are capable of freedom. As nations become corrupt and vicious, they have need of masters". Thomas Jefferson: *"The God who gave us life, gave us liberty at the same time. I have sworn upon the Altar of God, eternal hostility against every form of tyranny over the mind of man".*

Moving on, I will continue by means of illustrations using presidents as examples for my dissertation on the history of our Republic, its fall from grace, hence on a downhill passage, while still the greatest nation in the world. However, I submit I will continue to use them as examples. As a Republic we still have time although our opportunities grow slimmer, this to a great extent is affected by lack of, or interest in simple desire or a feeling of need.

Born on January 30, 1882, in Hyde Park, New York, Franklin D. Roosevelt was stricken with polio in 1921. He became the 32nd U.S. president in 1933, and was the only president to be elected four times. Also greatly expanded the powers of the federal government through a series of programs and reforms known as the New Deal. Roosevelt died in Georgia in 1945.

Franklin D. Roosevelt the president of our Republic arrived on the political scene in the early days of the depression, and generated a plight more appallingly injurious, to the people of our soveriegn states. This man instigated a war with Japan, aided by them and quickly added Germany and Italy, which on the whole certainly achieved one tricky obstruction, the overwhelming of a very deep depression. He had accomplished this event while at the cost of thousands upon thousands of American lives.

President Roosevelt joined the trio of Winston Churchill, Charles De Gaulle and Josef Stalin, thus creating a foursome to place together a quartet in order to defeat Adolf Hitler's infamous group of gangsters.

While in office, in order to arrive at his desired agendas, going so far as attempting to add four Judges to the U.S. Supreme Court. Although he was the only man truly popular with the people, regardless of his poor political activities voted him into office four times, the most of any man. I found no true achievements by this man to speak to, so I will move on.

Skipping along through Presidents Truman and Eisenhower, although President Truman reached a most difficult choice, by dropping the atomic bomb on Japan, therefore ending the war extremely quick, saving both American and Japanese lives. There was his famous statement, "the buck stops here".

Harry Truman (1884-1972), the 33rd U.S. president, assumed office following the death of President Franklin Roosevelt. In the White House from 1945 to 1953. Truman made the decision to use his influence to help rebuild post war Europe, worked to contain communism and regardless led the United States into the Korean War (1950-1953). He failed to heed the words of his general and so acting we now find ourselves in quite a dilemma, a truly severe challenge a true conundrum.

A Missouri native, Truman assisted in running his family farm after high school and served in World War I (1914-1918). He began his political career in 1922 as a county judge in Missouri and elected to the U.S. Senate in 1934. Three months after becoming vice president in 1945, the plain-spoken Truman ascended to the presidency. In 1948, he was reelected in an upset over Republican

Thomas Dewey. After leaving office, Truman spent his remaining two decades in Independence, Missouri, where he established his presidential library.

The term **Eisenhower Doctrine** Middle-east countries could request American economic assistance or aid from U.S. military forces if it was being threatened by armed aggression from another state. After which we engaged in three wars, lost all three and are bogged down in the Middle-east.

John F. Kennedy was the 35th President of the United States (1961-1963), the youngest man elected to the office. On November 22, 1963, when he was hardly past his first thousand days in office, JFK was assassinated in Dallas, Texas, becoming also the youngest President to die in office.

An inspiring John F Kennedy, a young man who served in the navy on a PT boat and received two medals for his heroism. As president it was his "Civil Rights Act" which we spoke of earlier and for a time quieted the issue of race relations. In the sphere of national relationships, his action for a time decreased tensions with Cuba. Sometime later the flawed activity called the Bay of Pigs, was a complete and utter failure.

In 1956 Kennedy almost gained the Democratic nomination for Vice President, and four years later was a first-ballot nominee for President. Millions watched his television debates with the Republican candidate, Richard M. Nixon. Winning by a narrow margin in the popular vote, Kennedy became the first Roman Catholic President. His Inaugural Address offered the memorable injunction: "Ask not what your country can do for you, ask what you can do for your country." As President, he set out to redeem his campaign pledge to get America moving again. His economic programs launched the country on its longest sustained expansion since World War II; before his death, he laid plans for a massive assault on persisting pockets of privation and poverty.

He wished for America to resume its old mission as the first nation dedicated to the evolution of human rights. Another program he began, the Alliance for Progress and the Peace Corps. President Kennedy brought American idealism to the aid of developing nations. However the rigid idealism of the Communist challenge remained paramount in his mind.

Shortly after his inauguration, Kennedy allowed an able group of Cuban exiles, thus already armed and trained, to invade their homeland. An attempt to overthrow the regime of Fidel Castro was a disaster. Soon thereafter, the Soviet Union restored its campaign contrary to an allied accord. Kennedy replied by reinforcing the Berlin stronghold and increasing our Nation's military strength, together with new efforts in outer space. Confronted by this response, Moscow, after this erection of the Berlin Wall, relaxed its pressure in central Europe.

In its place, the Russians now pursued the opportunity to install nuclear missiles on Cuban soil. When this was determined by air reconnaissance in October 1962, Kennedy executed a quarantine on all offensive weapons destined for Cuba. While the world trembled on the threshold of nuclear war, the Russians backed down and decided to remove the missiles. The American reaction to the Cuban crisis obviously persuaded Moscow of the futility of nuclear intimidation.

Kennedy now contended that both the U.S. and Russian sides had a vital interest in discontinuing the spread of nuclear weapons and slowing the arms race, a contention which led to the test ban treaty of 1963. The months after the Cuban near catastrophe showed meaningful progress toward his goal of "a world of law and free choice, banishing the world of war and coercion." Thus his administration now saw the beginning of new hope for both the equal rights of Americans and the peace of the world.

   While we were given a slogan "the war on poverty", instead of the war on poverty it was a war in Viet Nam. This war which we failed to win, cost immeasurable lives and treasure. Once again we the people, chose a man with considerable political power, but scarcely any character, in fact little more than a bombastic loud mouth from Texas. Regardless he created a law in the tax code, *which prevented Christians from speaking out against the government, nor support for any one candidate or another*. The law can be found in the IRS CODE- **501c3.** I stress the law creeped into existence by deceitful method and in view of the results, unconstitutional. This law would prevent churches if they spoke out, to claim a tax exempt status. This was accepted by Christians to this day, without a word of rightist or moral indignation. We find money the leading light here and of all places, Christian Churches. It is of course not my opinion, rather fact, nevertheless there is a sense of propriety involved, where the Christian churches could merely speak their awareness of the truth. There is more to the life of the bombastic sad individual, to what affect or reason. To think he replaced John Kennedy is reason to forget him.

   Then we the people were exposed to king Richard, tricky dickey Nixon, who finally ended our involvement in Viet Nam, surrendering after a tremendous loss of American life, not considering the Asians. However the king capitulated, removing himself from office in the face of impeachment, after which he swore "I'm no crook", nevertheless he was and the king was gone. We the people relinquished their God given rights, meekly whining to each other as to their plight.
Richard Nixon was elected the 37th President of the United States (1969-1974) after previously serving as a U.S. Representative and

a U.S. Senator from California. After successfully ending American fighting in Vietnam and improving international relations with the U.S.S.R. and China, he became the only President to ever resign the office of president, this as a result of the Watergate scandal.

As Vice President, Nixon took on major duties in the Eisenhower Administration. Nominated for President by acclamation in 1960, he lost by a narrow margin to John F. Kennedy. In 1968, he again won his party's nomination, and went on to defeat Vice President Hubert H. Humphrey and third-party candidate George C. Wallace.

His accomplishments while in office included revenue sharing, the end of the draft, new anticrime laws, and a broad environmental program. As he had promised, he appointed Justices of conservative philosophy to the Supreme Court. One of the most dramatic events of his first term occurred in 1969, when American astronauts made the first moon landing.

James Earl Carter Jr. is an American politician serving as the 39th President of the United States from 1977 to 1981. A member of the Democratic Party, he served as the Governor of Georgia prior to his election as president. Carter has remained active in public life during his post-presidency, and in 2002 he was awarded the Nobel Peace Prize. It is my opinion this man though failing to understand politics is nevertheless a true humanitarian.

Subsequently though his view was limited, in my judgement an ordinary man who professed being a Christian, he became known as, Jimmy Carter the peanut farmer. On November 4, 1979, a group of Iranian students stormed the U.S. Embassy in Tehran, taking more than 60 American hostages. The immediate cause of this action was President Jimmy Carter's decision to allow Iran's deposed Shah, who had been expelled from his country some months before, to come to the United States for cancer treatment.

Over the next decades, Carter built a distinguished career as a diplomat, humanitarian and author, pursuing conflict resolution in countries around the globe, as I have previously advocated, President Carter was a true and trusted individual all around the world.

The next emerging individual to arrive upon the scene was a contrast to some of the past incompetent and some unscrupulous persons, a man named Reagan. Ronald Reagan was an American politician and actor who was the 40th President of the United States, from 1981 to 1989.

This past movie star and an ex-governer of California was a relaxed man, who brought some recovery from the previous adverse personalities and their failed administrations. Among them were a few new and fresh ideas he brought with him, these helped to improve our economy and his sounder understanding of the Russian leaders. Thus this bold statement came about, "Mr. Gorbachev, tear down this wall", meaning the Berlin wall which had become a symbol of communist oppression, built in 1961.

Now we couple his actions with a Constitutional question over the infusion of the "Iran -contra" and corrupt clandestine action, never approved by the United States Congress. Despite denials from the President, Vice President George H. Bush, and other Reagan officials plus the CIA, never admitted having any involvement, nor had anything to do with the fighting in Nicaragua and funds which were never used covertly.

A Presidential investigation by journalists and Congress began to unravel the so-called Iran-Contra scandal. The scandal involved the secret sale of U.S. weapons to Iran (which was supposed to help in the release of U.S. hostages in the Middle East). It began in 1985, when the administration supplied weapons to Iran. This in his desire for securing the release of American hostages held by

Hezbollah terrorists, plus the failed Iran-Contra Affair, a war without the approval of Congress.

Dubbed the Great Communicator, the affable Reagan became a popular two-term president. He cut taxes, increased defense spending, negotiated a nuclear arms reduction agreement with the Soviets and is credited with helping to bring a quicker end to the Cold War. Reagan, who survived a 1981 assassination attempt, died at age 93 after battling Alzheimer's disease.

Then there was President George H. Bush Vice president to President Reagan. Remember the "read my lips" quote, this with his promise for no new taxes, of course that promise never materialized. Let's not forget the thousand points of light statements, I have only to speculate as to what that implied. In all fairness the economy was on the upswing at the time of the election, nevertheless it came a little too late.

Jennifer Fitzgerald, Olivia Pope and others were rumored to have been mistresses of George H. bush. This his wife had knowledge but chose to repudiate them. I have chosen to leave this matter to end here.

Bush's life revolved around and with his closest advisors and prominent critics, Thus First Lady Barbara Bush, (often called the boss). Those along with influential and formidable individuals, such as Condoleezza Rice, Colin Powell, Mikhail Gorbachev, etc.

It's possible he was qualified to lead our nation, rather he chose the wrong words at the wrong time, as "Read my lips". Thus President H. Bush words bit him and his election.

The preceding examples related to my assessments regarding the past presidents, is merely a reflection, a representation of the attitudes and an example by choice of the citizens, the people of our Republic.

Chapter Five

Here we visit the last three Presidents, relatively in more detail

This leads us to William Clinton and his two terms in the office of the Presidency, a mixture of beneficial sound policies and a base immoral damaging behavior. A man's shameless attitude with regards to his sexual activities while in office, this includes the past offices he held in Arkansas.

We shall begin with Billy Boy Clinton as a womanizer, a schoolboy obsesed with sex, past Governor of Arkansas. Clinton was born William Jefferson Blythe III on August 19, 1946, in Hope, Arkansas. He was the only child of Virginia Cassidy Blythe and traveling salesman William Jefferson Blythe Jr., who died in a car accident three months before his son's birth. In 1950, Virginia Blythe married car dealer Roger Clinton Sr. and the family later moved to Hot Springs, Arkansas. As a teen, Bill Blythe officially adopted his stepfather's surname. His only sibling, Roger Clinton Jr., was born in 1956, Bill's brother.

In 2001, Clinton became the first president to be married to a U.S. senator. Just days before he left office, first lady Hillary Clinton was sworn in as the freshman senator from New York. Hillary defeated an inexperienced young man from upstate New York, not unlike tossing raw meat to a tiger.

A short time later using convoluting words and meandering his way to the Presidency, not without the considerable assistance from his highly motivated, political wife Hillary. However, justifiably or not, due to his ability and past endeavors suited for the job, while he was skillful with negotiations, plus there were more women and easier to exploit. To the extreme he had swam too tricky, too long. Therefore he left office under a cloud of confusing failure, unstable for the position of President

This was somewhat as expected, near the finish he befittingly faltered as a result was impeached by the House of Representatives for lying under oath. This man being married to Hillary Rodman Clinton, a person so captivated and absorbed with politics her entire life, thus engaged while crafting Billy Boy's run for the Presidency, Hillary retained the presumption she was intended and anticipated her rise to the presidency. In my opinion, Hillary's more than 45 years in politics, had produced or created no creditable policy decisions, or commendable solutions. There were no true factual achievements whatsoever. Hillary was merely a primeval political creature, one of her own making, through self-importance and assumptions.

One would find her ambitious endeavors much needed for realignment, thus shifting her presumptuous persona forward on any popular program she could attach herself. Consequently it is my opinion her insufficiencies in character beyond being a caprices indulging wife, are bankrupt. Though being a wife also gives the impression she is only concerned of herself.

Furthermore, I imagine her philosophy coexisted non-transformed, or adjusted through all her time with political principles. It gives one the impression she had been radicalized in her young life and failed to grow past those premature thoughts.

While Bill Clinton was there for the beneficial joy of being in the limelight, though he was an intelligent politician with beneficial and appropriate concepts into the government for the good of the nation. All this, while he was quite a liar, philandering and adulterate womanizer. Preoccupations with women in his life had never transmuted or repaired from Arkansas to Washington D.C. all was joy and happiness, except many of the woman he raped or possessed.

In the end it was a young girl named Monica Lewinski and his lying concerning their sex life, which brought him to the end of his political position. The House impeached him and the Senate was close, rather they decided to maintain him as President while his final term was nearing the end. President Clinton was convicted of lying and fined more than $90,000

On the last day in office in January 2001, President Clinton agreed to a five-year suspension of his Arkansas law license as part of an agreement with the independent counsel to end the investigation. Clinton was automatically suspended from the United States Supreme Court bar as a result of his law license suspension. However, as is customary, he was allowed 40 days to appeal an otherwise-automatic disbarment. The former President resigned from the Supreme Court bar during the 40 day appeals period. These matters didn't end Bills involvement in political life, as I shall explain in detail later.

George Walker Bush born on July 6, 1946 American politician and served as Governor of Texas before coming President of the United States from 2001 to 2009. His term as Governor of Texas from 1995 to 2000. His education after graduating from Yale University in1968 was Harvard Business School in 1975. In May 1968, Bush was commissioned into the Texas Air National Guard. After two years of active-duty service, he was assigned to Houston's, Ellington field flying the Conair F 102's with the 147th Reconnaissance Wing.

Marrying Laura Welch in 1977, since it became a suitable time later, with her support, he ran and was elected president in 2000, after a close and controversial win over Democratic rival Al Gore, becoming the fourth President to be elected while receiving fewer popular votes than his opponent.

Soon after beginning his first term, on Sept. 11, 2001, two planes crashed into and destroyed the Twin Towers in New York City. This attack leaving behind more than three thousand dead Americans, including a shocked and grieving nation.

The airborne terrorist attacks on the World Trade Center, the Pentagon, and the thwarted flight against the White House or the Capitol building. All this on September 11, 2001, in which transformed George W. Bush into a wartime president. The attacks put on hold many of Bush's hopes and plans, and Bush's father, George H. Bush, the 41st president, declared that his son "faced the greatest challenge of any president". Then President Bush moved our military into Afghanistan as the "war on terrorism", then deployed troops to Iraq, this in order to find their possession of **weapons of mass destruction** as many world leaders assumed. After considerable search without finding any such weapons they were contemplating to finding . Although his bravado remained while his stating , "he was a warrior", this showed when landing on the aircraft carrier, Abraham Lincoln on which a banner read "Mission Accomplished" consequently the President went on to state that this was the end to major combat operations in Iraq.

President Bush's assertion soon twisted to bite him and quickly developed into a precipitous remark. Then almost immediately guerrilla warfare in Iraq increased, during which time he moved forward hard calling it a move of insurgency on Iraq. The vast majority of casualties, both military and civilian, occurred after his speech on the aircraft carrier stating, "Mission Accomplished".

Though the war in Iraq produced a Quasi Democratic Government, it was held together with fifteen thousand American troops, meanwhile Afghanistan was still in turmoil.

Thus in the meantime, at home Sandra Day O'Conner retired from the Supreme Court and President Bush replacement choice then became the appointment of John Roberts as Chief Justice of the Supreme Court. Rather this became quite an error in Bush's judgement. The economy was quite sluggish, inactive probably somewhat due to American military involvement in the middle-east, and his action on the lowering of taxes. For the duration of his time in office unemployment grew somewhat, from 4.2 to 6.3. It seemed that his perspectives and positions were at odds, leaving the people and our industries perplexed.

Another factor during his tenure was his lack of proclivity or of his need for concern, thus his weak response to the hurricane Katrina. President Bush approval ratings were as high as 90 % a few months after 9/11 and his actions in Afghanistan, then dropping to as low as 19% at the end of his presidency. Therefore on goes another eight years in our Republic's history. This was how I perceive the current times and aftermath, plus finding at: The Archives of *CBS News, C-Span, CNN, Assn. Press, New York Times* etc. and my study of books of our early history such as *What hath God Wrought* and Change to Chain.

Bush was challenged in his re-election bid in 2004 by Massachusetts Democratic Senator John Kerry. The election was a good contest, but Bush's contention that the invasion of Iraq had made the world more secure against terrorism, won the national political debate.

Bush was re-elected with 51 percent to 48 percent. Hence after the election, President Bush had these remarks for the nation on the inaugural stand, set the theme for his second term: "At this second gathering, our duties are defined not by the words I used, but by the history we have seen together. For half a century, America defended our own freedom by standing watch on distant borders.

After the shipwreck of communism came years of relative quiet, and then there came a day of fire. There is only one force of history that can break the reign of hatred and resentment, and expose the pretensions of tyrants, and reward the hopes of the decent and tolerant, and that is the force of human freedom tested but not weary… we are ready for the greatest achievements in the history of freedom."

A troubled economy also contributed to Americans' dissatisfaction with Bush. He began his presidency with a federal budget surplus; however, factors such as the enormous cost of fighting two wars and the broad tax cuts led to annual budget deficits starting in 2002. Then, in 2008, with America experiencing its worst financial crisis since the Great Depression, Congress passed a series of controversial Bush administration-sponsored plans to bail out the financial industry with hundreds of billions in federal funds. Bush also lobbied unsuccessfully for a plan to replace Social Security with private retirement savings accounts. Throughout his terms, Bush rarely wavered from his stance as a social conservative. He made two nominations to the U.S. Supreme Court, both in 2005: Chief Justice John Roberts (1955-) and Samuel Alito (1950-), both regarded as judicial conservatives.

Following the January 2009 presidential inauguration of Barack Obama, Bush left office as a polarizing figure. He and first lady Laura Bush returned to Texas, where they divided their time between homes in Dallas and Crawford. In 2010, Bush released a memoir, "Decision Points," in 2010, but otherwise maintained a low national profile.

After glimpsing into numerous presidential lives and their various activities, and after regarding a number of these recent and past individuals, we will close with the examination of Barack Obama, a person so occupied of himself it becomes difficult to articulate accurately the extreme and many facades in this man's greatly warped personality. I am astonished as how one person could stand in front of the American people, willfully and wantonly lie, so numerous times it's impossible to register. This in my opinion due to his being a pathological liar to the American people and in my opinion a megalomaniac.

He was born August 4, 1961, was an American politician who served as the 44th President of the United States from 2009 to 2017. He has deceitfully stated himself as a Negro and as the first African American to have served as president, untrue. Obama is in fact a mulatto, the fact remains Obama had a white mother, a socialist activist and social scientist Ann Dunham. She was born on November 29, 1942, in Fort Leavenworth, Kansas. His father was a Kenyan national recruited overseas on a college scholarship, and was reputed to be an opinionated, magnetic debater. He and Dunham soon began dating. Several months later, Dunham became pregnant. She and Barack Sr. were then married in a private ceremony on this date February 2, 1961. Then on August 4, 1961, Ann gave birth to a boy and named him Barack Obama, Jr. after his father.

President Obama's mother married his father at the ripe young age of 18, after the two met in a Russian-language class at the University of Hawaii. At the time, interracial marriage was illegal in most states. Dunham was three months pregnant when the two tied the knot. They divorced shortly thereafter, regardless Ann went to Indonesia by the time young Obama was six, he had moved there with his mother. However young Obama went to school and studied Kenyan ideas and philosophies, Ann and her son returned to Hawaii, while there he joined a gang. TA book describes his struggles as a young adult to reconcile social perceptions of his multiracial heritage. He wrote that he used alcohol, marijuana, and cocaine during his teenage years to "push questions of who I was out of my mind". I ask, why would he feel this need to join a gang and become involved in drugs. An older Obama was also a member of the "choom gang", a self-named group of friends that spent time together and occasionally smoked marijuana etc.

Much later while he was married to Michelle, the two went to Bali for seclusion in order that Barack could write his book "Dreams from my real father". A 1990 New York Times profile on Obama's election as Harvard's first black president caught the eye of agent Jane Dystel. She persuaded Poseidon, a small imprint of Simon & Schuster, to authorize a roughly $150,000 advance for Obama's proposed memoir. Rather he spent half and was forced to return the remaining funds.. Later Osnos the publisher met with Obama, took his word that he could finish the book, and authorized a new advance of $40,000, this book never stemmed by his hand, I sight this as part of his irrational, bizarre character.

However Bill Ayers wrote the book for Obama, thus his stating his being the author, was just another lie.

Once elected president of the Harvard Law Review more of a popularity contest than a literary one, Obama contributed not one signed word to the H.LR or any other law journal. As Matthew Franck has pointed out in the National Review Online, "A search of the Hein Online database of law journals, turns up exactly nothing credited to Obama in any law review anywhere at any time."

Then suddenly the media , one way or another meditated, then drooled all over Obama and transformed him from a laboring, but struggling, quite an unschooled amateur, with no paper trail beyond that of an unremarkable legal note and a poem about fig-stomping apes, into a "literary superstar".

Prior to 1990, when Barack Obama contracted to write Dreams from My Father, he had written very close to nothing, zero. Then, five years later, this untested 33 year-old produced what Time Magazine has called, with a straight face, "the best-written memoir ever produced by an American politician." All thanks to Bill Ayres also a Chicagoan.

Barack Hussein Obama at the age of 47 was elected the 44th president of the United States, sweeping away the last racial barrier in American politics with ease as the country chose him as its first Negro chief executive. This was also a lie as he was a mulatto.

Mr. Obama's election amounted to a national catharsis a repudiation of a historically unpopular Republican president and his economic and foreign policies, and an embrace of Mr. Obama's call for a change in the direction and the tone of the country. Rather it was "he would fundamentally transform America"

However it was just as much a strikingly symbolic moment in the evolution of the nation's fraught racial history, a breakthrough that would have seemed unthinkable just two years previously.

It was his second loss as Mr. Obama became president of the United States. Mr. Obama, 47, a first-term Democratic senator from Illinois, defeated Senator John McCain, Republican of Arizona, and a former prisoner of war who was making his second bid for the presidency.

Remembering how Obama, from the beginning gave away programs for persons unwilling to work, resulting in a hurtful manner for mostly Negroes. This had an obvious impact on the Negro male and hinderance for any improvements to our Republics' work force thus our overall economy. However it may have aided his intended political agenda.

In late August 1961, Obama's mother moved with him to the University of Washington in Seattle for a year. During which time, Obama Sr. completed his undergraduate degree in economics 1962, then left to attend graduate school on a scholarship at Harvard University. Obama's parents divorced in March. He visited his son in Hawaii only once, in 1971 before he was killed in an automobile accident in 1982, when Obama was 21 years old. In his early childhood, Obama recalled, "That my father looked nothing like the people around me, that he was black as pitch, my mother white as milk, which barely registered in my mind."- He later described his struggles as a young adult to reconcile social perceptions of his multiracial heritage. It seems yet then Obama had trouble with distinguishing reality with a fantasy.

In 1963, Dunham met Lolo Soetoro, at an Indonesian east-west center studying geography at the University of Hawaii, and the couple were married on Molokai on March 15, 1965.- After some years, this is where young Obama was schooled in Muslim ideas and Theology.

Mr.Obama became the first American from Hawaii and the first mulatto ever to be elected president of the United States, and Joe Biden became the first Roman Catholic ever elected vice president. McCain had secured the Republican nomination by March 2008, but the Democratic nomination was marked by a sharp contest between Obama and initial front-runner Senator Hillary Clinton, with Obama not securing the nomination until early June.

Nevertheless, Barrack Obama won and led our Republic in a disastrous direction. After his winning, he began to show himself as president, thus his statement of "fundamentally transforming The United States of America", and for eight years he superficially achieved his cleverest goal. McCain secured the Republican nomination but was a weak candidate for the Republican Party marked by a sharp contest between himself and Obama.

On November 4, lines at polling stations around the nation heralded a historic turnout and resulted in a Democratic victory, with Obama capturing some Republican strongholds (Virginia, Indiana) and key battleground states (Florida, Ohio) that had been won by Republicans in recent elections. Taking the stage in Chicago's Grant Park with Michelle and their two young daughters, Malia and Sasha, Obama acknowledged the historic nature of his win while reflecting on the serious challenges that lay ahead. "The road ahead will be long, our climb will be steep. We may not get there in one year or even one term, but America, I have never been more hopeful than I am tonight, I promise that we will get there. I promise you, we as a people will get there." Although he never accomplished that goal and broke countless other promises, plus lied so numerous times doing so knowingly and willfully.

The statement by Mayor Giuliani that he believed Obama "didn't love America". Nor do I think so, furthermore, I would add nor does he as a Muslim, have in the least, love for Christianity. However, any suggestion to this idea when thought as such and presented altogether as such, absolutely permits no option for a smidgen of success.

Since its stipulations persist, it is incumbent upon me to suggest an indispensable return to the simple principles of our Constitution. I stand baffled at the failure of Congress to act upon the impeachment of past President Obama, a man who has commited so many intentional lies and has failed to preserve, protect and defend our Constitution. Just the opposite fact, as he actually shamelessly trashed and shredded, instead of supporting the Constitution. In my opinion his desire was to abolish the Constitution plus any and all laws he deemed unnecessary or created laws as he wished. This doesn't exists in the minds of any rational individuals, rather he is an evil man, not worthy or should he allowed in any way to be trusted with any role within our Republic's government. Moreover it's sad we were exposed and subjected to his presence in any category whatsoever, in any case I question, why has this situation progressed without impeachment?

President Obama exhibits himself as prolific liar, when necessary echoes the same lie. This man who has commited so numerous premeditated lies knowingly and willfully, it's sad we have befallen and consented to such exposure as these corrupt manifestations. Nevertheless it's we the people that elected him into the office, it is we who are accountable.

One should by necessity, refocus their attention on the present difficulties now facing us and how we should oppose these confrontational, antagonistic positions. I am a strong adherent to the idea our constitution is not a living document, growing to satisfy a lethargic public while serving a ravenous government. I will indulge a new idea, refocusing my attention on the present complexities facing us at this very moment and how we should have confronted those adversities.

Returning to Jarrett, she had a key vote on Cabinet picks, as she opposed Larry Summers at Treasury and was among the first Obama aides to come around on Hillary Clinton at State. Again she had an immense say on ambassadorships and judgeships. She helped determine who gets invited to the First Lady's Box for the State of the Union, who may attend state dinners and bill-signing ceremonies, and who sits where at any of the above. This woman a hard core Muslim, wishing America to become a Muslim controlled entity.

It's just an assertion which has been passed along by many who have elected to postulate on this idea "let's keep up with the times", as this unfortunately is an argument poorly chosen. Provoking words spoken much earlier by men of remarkable wisdom, courage and that of comprehending the need for having faith in God, giving them the innermost spirit needed to struggle on and the audacity to take on the impossible. These were the men, the founders of our Republic and the fashioning of the greatest Constitution like none other, never before, or since. All under the guidance of God and with His blessing.

Today we are without these men, all the more so in our Christian society, they have chosen to ignore their knowledge, thus sadly ignoring that fire set to ignite future leaders by their example.

Below you will read some of their words. Words unspoken from many politicians or comprehended by few citizens of this era. Once again most people of this once inordinate Republic, the words chosen by men not abundantly found today, or if so, are not selected by the politicos and supported by the people. It seems we prefer to hear lies coming from the mouths of meager, destitute individuals, as we wish to hear bedtime stories rather than facing the truth. Please listen to a few words by wise men, far, far wiser than I.

As George Washington stated; *"Let us with caution indulge the supposition that morality can be maintained without religion. Whatever may be conceded to the influence of refined education, reason and experience both forbid us to expect national morality can prevail in exclusion of religious principle"*.

Other quote from the founders of our Republic, Benjamin Franklin, *"Only a virtuous people are capable of freedom. As a nation becomes corrupt and vicious, they have need of masters"*.

Thomas Jefferson; *"On every question of construction let us carry ourselves back to the time when the Constitution was adopted, recollect the spirit manifested in the debates, and instead of trying what meaning may be squeezed out of the text or invented against it, conform to the probable one in which it was passed".*

"To suppose that any form of government will secure liberty or happiness without any virtue in the people is a chimerical idea". James Madison

"The sum of it... "is, if we would most truly enjoy the gift of Heaven, let us be a virtuous people; then shall we both deserve and enjoy it. If failing we shall not enjoy it, though the form of our constitution carries the face of the most exalted freedom, in reality become the most abject slaves". Samuel Adams

We find Senate Republicans were attempting to ascertain how former Secretary of State Hillary Clinton's top assistant Huma Abedin, was allowed to keep working at the State Department under a special part-time status, while also being employed at a politically-connected consulting firm, according to evidence. This action by her is illegal, why is she still operating as such, where is our congress, why are they idle?

Hillary's private Internet server and email accounts. They were never meant for such, they were to be used for supposed State Department correspondence, just as those that were considered confidential and classified, still this server was defined improper to use. Senator Grassley claims that the earlier requests were sent to the department and have largely been ignored, however the Senate was then controlled by the Democrats. Now with the GOP in the majority new requests have gone to the department's inspector general and to Secretary of State John Kerry, seeking resolution. Their I await, as that request will also die a certain death. Correspondingly what obstructions made it difficult, was the fact that during Clinton's time as Secretary of State, her department was without an Inspector General for quite a long period of time. Grassley's first probe began in 2013, he requested all communications in relation to the Abedin incident, after she went from being a full-time assistant chief of staff for Clinton to a part-time assistant chief of staff. The reason for the changes was that Huma began her job with the government consulting company, Tenneco.

Meanwhile Senate Republicans were renewing efforts to learn why Huma Abedin, a top assistant to Secretary of State Hillary Clinton, why she was allowed to stay at the agency under a special part-time status, moreover being employed at a politically-connected consulting firm.

So trusting when the new requests arrive, they would have greater impact on Secretary of State John Kerry, therefore by seeking a far deeper involvement, Grassley is expecting it to give rise to sounder conclusions plus expecting pronounced solutions. My opinion, as for knowledge pertaining to the people, the unknown will remain as an unknown, no tangible results shall transpire, expecting zero answers. All this as our President Obama continued to sleep on these episodes.

Now disasters wrought by the compromise of military and diplomatic intelligence sent and received through Hillary Clinton's unsecured private email server. In the meantime past president Obama is involved in interpolation to the Mexican border crossing, sympathetic to their dilemma. Therefore he designed a program for their Catch-22, called "The Dreamers". Nevertheless, our girl Abedin at the age of two, moved with her family, her mother Syed Zainul Abedin and Saleha Mahmood Abedin her father both Muslims to Saudi Arabia, where she was raised until returning to the United States for college. Now Abedin is close to the Muslim Brotherhood where her brother is a member of the brotherhood. We all remember her husband, as she was married to **Anthony Weiner** the sex pervert, Democrat poster boy ex U.S. House Member. Further she was Sect. Hillary Clinton's closest confidant up to and including the election for the presidency. Again we found Obama out in the heather lands selling his idea of health care insurance, which began failing from its beginning.

   This lovely lady was raised Muslim and continues to practice the religion even though her husband Weiner is Jewish and a social media sexual exhibitionist and woman hunter. In addition to English, she also speaks Urdu (the national language of Pakistan) and Arabic (the official language of Saudi Arabia). Only my opinion, but I find it a rather curious situation, this Muslim woman and a sex exhibitionist Jew are integrated, wow

   Obama and Janet Napolitano appointed devout Muslim to Homeland Security Post, Arif Alikhan from the Muslim brotherhood as Assistant Secretary for Policy Development. Source of the announcement: Homeland Security Press Room. How could this occur?

 Kareem Shira, who was born in Damascus Syria was appointed by DHS Secretary Napolitano, as Homeland Security Advisory Council (HSAC) Washington, DC. June 5, 2009. Once again why again Muslin?

The American-Arab Anti-Discrimination Committee (ADC) was proud to announce at a ceremony held in Albuquerque, New Mexico, DHS Secretary Janet Napolitano swore-in ADC National Executive Director Kareem Shira as a member of the Homeland Security Advisory Council (HSAC). The questions are persistently unchanged, why?

Why are devout Muslims being appointed to critical Homeland Security positions? Was it not men of the "Devout Muslim Faith" that flew planes into two buildings in New York, not too long ago? What the heck is this President thinking? It is my personal opinion

Obama knows precisely what he was embarking upon, as he, himself is a Muslim.

Arif Ali khan is the Deputy Executive Director for Homeland Security Law Enforcement and Fire/EMS at Los Angeles World Airports. He was appointed to the new position in October 2011 and is responsible for the 1,200 sworn police officers and civilian security officers that protect Los Angeles International Airport, Ontario International Airport, and the Van Nuys Airport. DHS head Janet Napolitano appointed Ali khan , Assistant Secretary for Policy Development. Imam Mohamed Magid naturalized citizen who immigrated to the United States from the Sudan in 1987.

In 2011 President Barack Obama appointed Magid to serve in a *"Countering Violent Extremism, Working Group"* with the DHS. On January 22, 2013 Magid took part in the inaugural ceremonies of President Obama but the White House has no Sharia Czar, a title given to Iman Magid by members of the Obama Administration. In 2007 Alikhan was instrumental in removing the Muslim terror tracking plan in LA. The Muslim 'Mapping' Plan of the Los Angeles Police Department is now "dead on arrival" according to Chief William Bratton. "It is over and not just put on the side". One would expect that's a fact.

Chief Bratton in a meeting with the Muslim leadership of Southern California, at that time was moderated by Arif Alikhan. Chief Bratton acknowledged the hurt and offense caused to Muslims and agreed to send a letter to the Muslim community announcing the official termination of the 'mapping' plan.

"I would be very worried, both for the United States and its friends in the region, like Israel, about the implications of any substantial involvement by ElBaradei in setting Egyptian national policy," warns John Bolton, the former United States Ambassador to the United Nations, who had extensive dealings with the Egyptians as a U.N. official.

El Baradei headed the U.N's International Atomic Energy Agency, or I.A.E.A., for 12 years. It was in that role that some accused him of being biased toward Iran, though he denied it. He had a stormy relationship with the George W. Bush administration, which tried to block his reappointment as head of the agency in 2005.

Critics accused ElBaradei of sometimes seeming to give Tehran the benefit of the doubt, and downplaying a possible military aspect to its nuclear program despite what the U.S. and others said was evidence to the contrary.

Less than a year and a half ago, ElBaradei told the Council on Foreign Relations in New York, that "we have no indications, no concrete proof that Iran has an ongoing nuclear weapons program and that is my view".

Then critics, like former Ambassador Bolton, fault him. "He is one of those fashionable anti-American international leftists. He's already criticized the United States for its policy in Egypt this week, and he announced in his previous presidential campaign. Stating he would recognize Hamas and end sanctions against Hamas, which presumably means opening the Egyptian border with the Gaza Strip. He has also said the Muslim Brotherhood in Egypt is not an extremist organization.

But the inspector told Bolton, Mohamed ElBaradei believed that as top U.N. official, he had a moral responsibility to be objective, and impartial no matter what the critics say. ElBaradei now shed the role as he marches with protestors on the Cairo streets.

Cairo Hamas and Muslim Brotherhood are all terrorists, along with their 100 front organizations. Just google "the project Muslim Brotherhood" for the truth and facts. The Islam Caliphate will eventually come to America, unless moral worthy men and women prevent it from happening. It is impossible today to tell any difference between so called peaceful Islam and peaceful

Mosques since there is none, due to the practice of "Taqivya" that is found in the Quran. A lie if told with a good intent, or to protect Islam, it is worthy. If anyone can describe the difference, please let me be given the details. One should be able to express themselves on religious matters, without a need of a lie.

We have yet to learn from the tragedy of 9/11. After over sixteen years of violence and terror from Islam, the matter has not been resolved. Ayaan Hirsi Ali perhaps said it best, "Violence is inherent in Islam". It must be noted that Ayaan has won every single debate on the subject as to whether or not Islam is a religion of peace. It is not. She speaks from experience as a former Muslim, and speaks out against radical Islam and Sharia Law. She has been accused of hate speech and has death threats on her life, merely for telling the truth.

Taqiyya is one of the reasons we are "surprised" by acts of violence or terror from those previously considered of being a "moderate" Muslim, if there is such a character.
Obama is the prototype of a paradigm of such an individual, if one to such a degree could possibly exist

Why he was even allowed back into the United States with his known terrorist connections, and why was he not arrested let alone teaching at a college? He apparently has convinced the government that he is a moderate Muslim, (will we never learn that for Islamic ideas it's OK to lie, their own words ?). Google "the project Muslim brotherhood" their doctrine to destroy America from within by stealth jihad, lies and deception just like Anwar Awlaki, who had the majority of our government convinced, he was just a moderate Muslim. Anwar Awlaki, the leader of Al Qaeda was killed in a drone attack and it was authorized by President Obama on 9/20 2011. Obama was without choice, thus this action, brother killing brother, as Cain and Able, not so unusual.

The recent release of the 5 Taliban Terrorist leaders will cause more Americans to die as they continue to plot another 9/11 where they left off. It seems just one more injudicious decision by our government, it will be the major mistake currently of the government, to have released these savage Taliban "monsters". This while more Americans will die as a direct result of this pitiable decision, in a multitude of destitute catalogue of his selections, he has preferred.

This by deliberate action, past President Obama, who should be impeached for his past treasonous proceedings, now we face another. I could mention our "open borders" that are bringing in more terrorists daily, to eventually attack us, but that's entirely another subject.

Al Qaeda and the Taliban are alive and well, creating havoc throughout the World. How many more people will be slaughtered by them? It is another Holocaust killing of innocent children, and infidels, Christians, Jews, and priests, and anyone that stands in their way of the Caliphate. There were over 1.3 million Christians in Iraq, Iran, Syria, Egypt and Lebanon, now there are less than 300,000.

Where is the World tumult and condemnation of these barbaric, killer savages? They must be stopped now. Why aren't "We the People" pressing the Congress we placed in office, the need to respond to the fundamentals which are identified appropriately by the actions of these barbarians, deposited directly in front of the congress, this includes Barack Obama. This vile man was acting out his best to provide the Iranians with nuclear weapons. As Sect. of State Kerry flies from place to place, actually he was only globetrotting, as negotiations seemed to have grown more complex as each day passed.

Furthermore, why have Christians become absent, worst comatose, I persist in asking, where is our faith in God Almighty,

He will not fail us if we are down on our knees. We may seek another, but there is no other answer, only God

In my simple and even so basic a mind for examining foreign affairs, nevertheless, discovered in my unrestrained judgement that of Obama's pathological mentality, coming from an uncontrolled person shall bring chaos to America and to our reliable and trustworthy allies, the Israelis. We should have acted more quickly as time was presently more transitory than we might have assumed.

I am of the opinion, better yet convinced that we must begin again and return to God as were our founders believed and were followers of God. Now as the situation grows far worse, which requires greater measures on the part of Christians and especially Christian leaders, it is incumbent upon those who say they are Christians to pick up the pace, take the necessary measures by pressing their elected representatives, not to accept the negotiations in any way, whatsoever with Iran. I encourage you to remember this, our nation was built on the separation of powers and congress being one, thus regrettably I do not trust Congress to act in respect to the injurious nature and actions of the past on by Obama without pressure from the people.

As citizens of this nation, a nation designed on the idea that a union of many diversified states, yet each sovereign could work together, for the benefit of each other. I am still certain this is true, thus believing this design was inspired by God, hence will not fail if properly administered. It is an indisputable fact, there are millions of citizens who think and have faith in the same God. We by choice have chosen leaders in congress who must support these ideals and are obliged to meet their task, we are masters

It is as we the people, who essentially are the impetus that is necessary to perform this required action, for the reversal of direction this nation of ours ought to travel. We cannot wait for some luminary or superstar. In fact nor anyone else who may happen along and then by some mysterious means guide us through the Nile River and leading us out of captivity, figuratively speaking. Let's face it, there was only a few who believing He would assist them in their efforts to acquire their security and freedom from England's King George.

Hence the weakness of Bible believing Christians of which I reason, have allowed this true incursion of disarray to have existed. Furthermore, I have reflected over my own thinking and am able to see the unequivocal lack of our faith in God and a noticeable reduction on our reliance in Him. This living within a nation conceived by Godly men, to whom followed His precepts, thus creating this unique Republic of ours.

We have experienced a venture through our history, woefully a mere seventy five years and our priorities had fallen away, succumb to a man using the Negro to advance his personal agenda. Thus we are now reaching into today, including our current trials, anxieties and the wide ranging difficulties facing our nation. The deterioration of our society, in most cases without a feeling for the necessity for change, yet poverty, deprivation and failure is at an extraordinary daunting high, from which to mend and restore plus put back together our righteous position.

Except for greed and hunger for power, the nation could have been that proverbial beacon on the hill. Instead we find ourselves being starved for trust by our friends and deprived of fear by our enemies, immeasurably to our demise.

In this short dissertation I have endeavored to demonstrate how easily man is corrupted, perhaps not necessarily money or power, though our desires for more, bigger and better things are a great weakness, it seems we all enjoy and to some extent having worked for them, feel they are fair game, thus perhaps it's the overdoing we have indulged ourselves. However we are obligated to a commitment for reversing ourselves and demand government to do likewise, remembering they are our servants, as it was they who were begging to serve.

A moment ago I spoke of Chief Justice John Roberts and his propensity for deceit, costing the citizens of the nation multi-billions of dollars and contributing to the social decline of our republic and are still reeling from the impact. Thomas Jefferson once stated in the Declaration of Independence *"when a long train of abuses and usurpations, pursuing invariably the same object evinces a design to reduce them under absolute despotism, it is their right, it is their duty, to throw off such government, and to provide new guards for their future security. Such has been the patient sufferance of these* colonies"*, one could easily exchange colonies to states, as it appears we are at that point.

These colonists were willing to defy England, going to war over similar difficulties, taxation without proper representation, inflicting their preferences, loss of liberty and uttermost, losing their freedom of choice to worship as they pleased. Sound anything similar to you at this point?

I have read the transcripts of the following cases involved around The Affordable Care Act and the arguments presented by the government (defendants) and by the plaintiff's listed below.

The following arguments I had undertaken some years ago, I find it reasonable and appropriate to once again use these arguments in this little book to illustrate a corrupt government, at its highest level. The so called "Affordable Care Act", truly developed into a contrary system, therefore a waste, a conceived scheme and merely a scam, meant to help and support the Insurance Corporations. An example is shown next.

Case 11- 393 *National Federation of Independent Business, et al., , v. Kathleen Sebelius, Secretary of Health and Human Services, et al.,*

Case 11- 398 *Department of Health and Human Services, et al.,v. Florida, et al.*

Case 11-400 *Florida, et al., v. Department of Health and Human Services, et al.*

All three of these cases make up the authentic fundamentals of which the Affordable Care Act was argued, thus heard by the Supreme Court of the United States, verdict in June of 2012. I have established my facts and presented by *"Fiat Justitia ruat coelom",* after a long and exanimating study, therefore using their own offered and existing court cases against them, plus simple logic using the true meaning of words which they had used.

Again our national government in a case concerning subsides, to be used by individuals in a State exchange, to help individuals in need of assistance. For better clarity and simplicity, the law is observed and explained in italics.

This found in the following portion of the act: **HEALTH PLAN, A PART OF SECTION 1401 (Generally called subsides)** *At (2), (A):*

> (1) IN GENERAL. *The term premium **assistance** credit amount' means, with respect to any taxable year, the sum of the premium assistance amounts are determined under this paragraph with respect to all coverage*

months of the taxpayer occurring during the taxable year.

(2) PREMIUM ASSISTANCE AMOUNT A premium assistance amount determined under this subsection with respect to any coverage month is the amount equal to the lesser of—

*(A) the monthly premiums for such month for 1 or more qualified health plans offered in the **individual market within.***

*(B) **a State** which cover the taxpayer, the taxpayer's spouse, or any dependent (as defined in section 152) of the taxpayer and which were enrolled in through an*

***Exchange established by the State** under 1311 of the Patient Protection and Affordable Care Act.*

*The Supreme Court misstated that the Congress misplaced a few words and there were drafting errors rather there were none such as those words. **Individual markets within a State**, and one could add **Exchange established within a State**, please note the capital S used in this statue, specifically denoting one of the fifty States which were enrolled in State exchanges, these words sound clear to me.*

There were no drafting errors, no misplaced words. Only these architects reached a reckless, strategic decision, their dangling of federal subsidies as the reward for a State assuming the costs of running an exchange. The ploy was adverse, excessive and risky.

Though if successful, it would allow the feds to unload the cost of exchanges to the states, while state politicians could claim credit for reducing the sticker shock of the insurance in its markets. So Oklahoma and 35 other states just weren't interested. The fact is Obama got exactly what he wanted and had planned, no exceptions, only it didn't go as they had pre-planned. So now it was up to the Supreme Court to fix the problem, and they did what was necessary, the law and the Constitution be dammed. This corrupt reasoning, without Constitutional law or ideology is called "Judicial Deference", an idea brought into the courts after Chief Justice Marshall's decision in 1803 concerning the Marbury vs Madison case.

Jefferson's statement regarding such ideology. I am paraphrasing, "warning *not to attempt to expand the meaning of the law, keep it in the spirit and time it was written, plus never attempt squeezing it in order to get beyond the form in which it was intended."* Food for thought, again from Thomas Jefferson, *"I tremble for my country when I reflect that God is just, that His justice cannot sleep forever".*

Which brings me to the next case I question, with their decision released the following day after hearing same, hence the same sex marriage issue, being passed with a five to four outcome. This in favor of preventing the states from stopping or impeding same sex marriage. Strange that now Justice Roberts is choosing the absolute opposite position, he now is of the opinion that the law must be followed, Amendments Nine and Ten (state rights) as this is paramount and failing to do so would be unconstitutional.

The results of these two Supreme Court decisions will reverberate through the core of our Christian Republic, bringing new grief and additional distress hereafter to an overburdened populace. Furthermore moving farther away from God and the need to follow His moral standards, which will bring about a significant detrimental change and decline to our nation.

However, I remain commited to my premise, again I state it's the people who are the government, without the people there is no government, as it is us who select our House Members, from our immediate area within our state, for the period of two years. Then we select two Senators, people from our particular state who serve six years. Now we have in Washington and are known as the nonelected individual persons, while we have seen a consequence emerging into our lives, it's imminently more so. I have become alarmed and somewhat worried blaming Saul Alinsky, though he deftly outlined the methods. While the original bureaucracy of the federal government consisted only of employees from these three small departments, State, Treasury, and War. The executive branch today employs almost three million people. Not only have the numbers of bureaucrats grown, but also the methods and standards for hiring and promoting people have changed dramatically. I'm about to blame those elected officials who are so stupid as to comply with unelected organizations, for the sake of what? Money, power, awards, junkets, etc. Elected officials are doing things which are antithetical to their oaths of office and their numerous responsibilities to the voters. Why and how? And yes, I blame the voters perhaps more, for allowing this and electing all the wrong people to office.

Returning to the original premise of this little book, my ability in some simple manner explaining our early history, to the exposing of government corruption at its highest level, the Supreme Court of the United States. This exercise bringing to bear the profound willingness of government to defraud, deceive and betray in order to maintain the will of Congress and/or the President, as today the three branches of government are united as one. Creating the loss of freedom, liberty and sovereignty for the states and its people. This situation didn't come about without the assistance of the people to facilitate a so called democracy, actually socialism with an opportunity to vote for which socialist, now the entire Democratic Party is just that, socialistic, this ideology is where you have no clear choice. While this delusional Hillary Clinton appearing to brings us numerous reasons for her loss, of course none of her own. Hillary's who lost of the election was merely a very poor candidate, Then stated she believes the electoral college needs to be abolished, she states she received more votes thus won the election.

Therefore, it brings into view the real fact, it's the people and the Constitution which ultimately define how our government functions and chooses how a nation moves forward, or more often retreats into chaos. The lack of these facts are to my mind, are obviously pointing toward absolute socialism, though many of our time-consuming, prolonged engagements in the polititical system, cry conservatism, rather their detectible actions prove their interest to be otherwise, self- tolerance. Please remember this is not a Democracy but a Republic.

The exposure of these facts are the lack of people's interest, each citizen to profit, if having some involvement, even drawing on a small portion in their government and I will again say, especially those who call themselves Christian people. It is not enough to spout the name of Christ and fail to lead in the effort to maintain our Republic, as it was originally designed by God and wise men. At least recognizing the God of Christianity and installing His' values into our Constitution. Therefore given this republic a Christian basis, the foundation on which to build this young nation. Meanwhile people were free to conduct themselves, with liberty, freedom and pursuit of happiness as they so decide.

The most important belief, being our faith in God Almighty, strange as it may seem, since He is our only redeeming strength and simply the solitary answer to the nation's degeneration, both as individual society and the elected political creatures leading us into chaos. We being Christians are obligated to pray for God's guidance and that again our people will begin believing in support from God. As astute men, who with God's wisdom and strength, crafted this once great Christian Republic, the preamble exemplifies these sharp ideas and considerations for the soveriegn states purpose of joining together in unification. We need once again reach for those ideals and gather them into our Republic and its people.

"We the People of the United States, in Order to form a more perfect Union, establish Justice, insure domestic Tranquility, provide for the common defense, promote the general Welfare, and secure the Blessings of Liberty to ourselves and our Posterity, do ordain and establish this Constitution for the United States of America".

These simple words were all which were necessary and essential for an explanation of the following Constitution of the United States, our Republic as a Christian sovereign body of persons.

James Madison, the fourth president, known as The Father of Our Constitution made the following statement *"We have staked the whole of all our political institutions upon the capacity of mankind for self-government, upon the capacity of each and all of us to govern ourselves, to control ourselves, to sustain ourselves according to the Ten Commandments of God."* Stating once again Patrick Henry, that patriot and Founding Father of our country said, *"It cannot be emphasized too strongly or too often that this great nation was founded not by religionists but by Christians...not on religions but on the Gospel of Jesus Christ".*

These words are all fundamental and were indispensable to bring into being a Christian republic of Christian sovereign states in harmony. While the States arrived upon the concept, of a belief and view in a secular government, it would be driven by the people and of the people. It came from people of Christian faith and practices and ideology, as there was none other. Their only diversities were minor opinions as how they would exercise their faith in God and Jesus Christ.

It is long past time for Christians of all denominations to gather together in order to challenge our House members and Senators to restore the inspirations and beliefs given us for a secure Christian Republic in order to sustain our future.

I firmly believe and have faith God will assist if we as a people will turn to Him for support, as He is familiar with our need for help. As stated in the Declaration of Independence, *we are endowed by our creator with unalienable rights, which among them are Life, Liberty and the pursuit of happiness.* Please note the word pursuit, happiness is not a given, rather one must pursue, these rights are granted but as individuals we need to work toward them. As a result we are the government, we need to work at keeping it wholesome and unadulterated as humanly possible. I am guaranteed by God, if we chose to be an enthusiast of His thoughts and designs for our future in this life, we will flourish by accomplishments we only dream
Therefore it is my desire for you to take away from the following exercise, intended for you to contemplate. In so doing, hoping you find how our government has acquired power they were never granted. However it is the facts, the truth as they have no proclivity for truth. Their function is to support congress and their legislation regardless of how it may affect the people. Within the cases you will discovery all the necessary information to support my contentions, cases to read and where to find them.

One last concept to meditate upon, President Trump for all his bombastic remarks, has yet to remove habeas corpus**, or i**mprison judges, or the media which hates and scorns him, the individuals who disagree with him are not sent to jail. What's more I have yet to observe a start of war against governors concerning State sovereignty, where 650,000 lives were lost. Then again he has shown compassion for the Negro. Yet there is a memorial for the man who commited all these ruthless atrocities and more.

Chapter Six

The Supreme Court's Notion of the Hypothesis of Equivalence. This Warped Theory with a Perverted View of our Republic, thus the U.S. Supreme Court has become an accurate and perfect example of corruption.

Researching the subject, plus illustrating the corruptness of our government at its upmost level, is the United States Supreme Court. In fact the arrogance and total disregard for the citizens of our Republic is without equal. Their absence and denial for support of the Constitution, is overwhelming in the Affordable Care Act, (Obama Care) other than perhaps their misuse of same. The case histories used by Chief Justice John Roberts were so lacking in backing and assistance to his claims, I found, if it had not been so important an issue, his words and examples would have come about amusing. Nonetheless, the desire for calmness and self-assurance for the citizens, speaks a volume regarding the true interest in their government. It is without question led to the chaos we now find ourselves. Convenience to deceiving, spurious and dishonest activities, seems the court found solace in participating.

The Court's misguided desire for defense of the Congress in this case was pure patronage, thus becoming a benefactor to this scam and hoax. This situation is similar to the case of subsides for persons in State Exchanges, simply unadulterated lies and the self-reliance for corruption, this was actuality and truthfully, fundamentally a scam.

Thus, Chapter six is no less positive than Chapter One, just simple facts, then facts are of a stubborn nature and difficult to accept, in any event remain true. I am going to use a court like platform, in Latin "minor se marjoram dexterity".

I have devoted more than six months researching these case histories plus their words the court used and their true meaning, again time spent to study the transcripts of the court in each case. This in addition to their spoken words, perhaps better stated their misspoken words.

This following trial shall thoroughly and likewise equally applied to these cases 11-393, 11-398, 11-400 heard by the Supreme Court, as a trial called *"In fraudem legis"* , or "Tria capita" both Latin, nevertheless their meaning is appropriate, *In fraud of the law, with intent of, or view of evading the law.*
This exercised by government was counter to our citizen's freedom and family rights. All these thoughts and words become the nature of this trial and are well correlated to the case presented, counter to the Supreme Court decision, Chief Justice John Roberts presiding.
However I will proceed with my positions in truth, even as a mock trial, therefore in my presentation of facts as to those persons so involved actually charged by myself with their own words.

George Melcher… Citizen of New Mexico, Petitioner

Cases in question

Patient Protection and Affordable Care Act and Other Things.   I.R.S. code 1986-at 5000A

The following Cases- doc., 11-393, 11-398, 11-400

Vs

Chief Justice Roberts, and

Justices Ginsburg, Breyer, Sotomayor, Kagan

My Opening Remarks

After reading and trying to assimilate the Supreme Courts' faulty evaluation regarding the Patient Protection Affordable Care Act, unfortunately a misuse of congresses taxing power, thus inappropriately becoming an exaction. This is not within the taxing powers of the congress so enumerated in our Constitution. Thus stated in Article One section eight.

As a consequence, for myself as a Christian patriot a need to challenge our government, under the authority of the First Amendment section four, *"to petition the government for a redress of grievance"*, I found the Supreme Court especially the Chief Justice John Roberts, among others of that supposed august body, clearly and obviously culpable and liable. It has become apparent and necessary, that someone challenge or at the very least, questions as to the foundation for the mandate, the power to tax, which becomes the very heart of the mandate of this act. Case doc.no.11-393, 11-398, 11-400, the IRS code 1986 or one in the same, found and explained at 5000A in the previously named 1986 code IRS manual, Title 26.

As a result of our administration's duplicity and its many absolute destructive actions, even while deceit prevails, we have taken upon ourselves the chore of exposing the illegitimacy of the actions of individual persons. Passing laws which we the people are the recipients, laws of endless debt, hostile to our future, our children's, and perhaps our children's children.

Having taken this task as a citizen, to become bold and audacious enough to challenge five of the nine supposedly wise persons in the Supreme Court of these United States, our Republic. As a result I have ascertained flaws, weakness and in record positions, outright deception.

Thus, for the most part I found it demanding of the truth to be conveyed, brought forward to the people. As the unscrupulous Nancy Pelosi stated *"you must first past the bill* (the Affordable Care Act)" so *you will understand it, in this fog of politics."* I found that statement a ludicrous and incredible statement, by a woman drawn to lies.

Now some several *years* later we are wiser. Not one representative read the appalling new law, 2700 plus pages, urgently pressed for passage by representative from California's eighth district, Ms. Pelosi.   Is my existence as a citizen not sufficient to be so bold as to ask why? While sitting there from her socialist perch, she drove the House of Representatives, many perhaps were merely concerned with their political positions. While they were only interested in setting their future for the game of wild animals, mules vs. elephants. They promised this bill would be posted on the internet for 72 hours, of course I knew this was a fabrication.

 So without ado I printed a copy of all 2700 plus pages and sure as the sun rises in the east, less than 24 hours, puff it was gone, like smoke from a slow burning ember.

  Then our imaginative Supreme Court had found a spurious way to perform the task presented them, without a whimper from the American people, including the Christian faithful, except for Justice Scalia, Kennedy, Thomas and Alito. Consequently, there goes our Christian republic deeper into socialism, devoid of a simple moan or a whimper, no one expectant of a large challenge by Christianity. The ideology of the program is in itself pure socialism.

It is my firm belief, as a true citizen of New Mexico, one of fifty sovereign states, I deem and have faith that my duty as a Christian patriot was to challenge Chief Justice John Roberts decision on those cases before them. I have found errors, lies and deception and truth stretching at its very best. His case law abstractions to Justice Marshall a Federalist, were used numerous times, yet none were used accurately or applicable.

Justice Marshall served from 1801 - 1835 and was instrumental in bringing the courts into a more equal status with the other two branches of government thus bringing a full concept of the government.

That being said, however he (John Roberts) moved the body politics to the liberal point of view, far from the ideas of Thomas Jefferson. The selection of the seat of the National government was chosen from, (*soveriegn persons which were elected from soveriegn states and sent to area of ten sq. miles*). Then these persons came to this area called Washington D.C., creating an area to exchange ideas and hopefully helpful and necessary information. Not a retreat from their state government, nevertheless leading to the creation of separation between the states and the United States' government, all this happening with the loss of states and people's sovereignty.

Strangely this was where John Roberts was most comfortable in States case law, few federal or use of Constitutional law, inexplicable thinking for that of Justice. I found his use of positives while proving negatives, very disturbing. His ability to use the narrowest of rules, even thinning them out further, trying to prove his point, most often devoid of any reason or a Constitutional parallel.

This nation was founded on the principles established by God, as quoted in the document which gave validation for the creation of our Constitution, the Declaration of Independence. A phrase most often used, Life, Liberty and the pursuit of Happiness, the twelve preceding words are regularly forgotten words, they are absolute, "endowed by their creator with certain unalienable rights, that AMONG them are"… Life, Liberty and the pursuit of Happiness.

I wish to quote from James Madison *"Each state in ratifying the constitution, is considered a sovereign body independent of all others, and only to be bound by its own voluntary act. In this relation then, the new constitution will, be a republic and not a national constitution."*

I'm sorry but today it's evolving into a diminishing discard, nevertheless it lays there waiting for honest people to support and for government to comply with and acquiesce. Question, are we ready to see this event again come to fruition?

Finally I expect to demonstrate how Justice Roberts brings into play a convoluted version of case law, in addition excessive bloviation to the point of great redundancy. Likewise his constant obstruction by the twisting of words and terms. This case isn't the subject of tax laws, but rather the Affordable Care Act, not of Health Care either, rather essentially an agenda with regards to insurance. All else is abstract bloviation, rhetorical at best, or pure political lies, probably both in conjunction. Though my trial is presented as a similitude, in Latin (minor se marjoram dixerit) it is scrupulously factual and genuine. Although one cannot prosecute these Justices, or impeach them at this time, they are as I have asserted, and will prove them to be guilty of corruption plus acting as charlatans. Most all are guilty and have become a part of the tradition of our current corrupt government. Therefore turning on a phrase called *Judicial Deference,* focused not on law, merely on the choice of words meaning as they arbitrarily declare them and not necessarily at all as Noah Webster's definition, even to the point of converting the law through this action, therefore fitting their issue into this particular occasion. These mindsets have no legal grounds, simply without the ability to substantiate or able to corroborative with laws. Merely an off ramp from our Constitution attempting to convert it into a worthlessly designed document, a powerless instrument, yet it is still a powerful consortium of words, given us by God through wise men, designed to be governed by people chosen from a confederation of individuals, for a selected period of time.

I pray God these unscrupulous activities will change soon, bringing hope for our Republic and for the verbose deception by those persons, indicated by name in the following paragraph.

At this point I will place on trial, actually a simulated trial, one Chief Justice Roberts, and Justices Ginsburg, Breyer, Sotomayor and Kagan. This, as I firmly believe will demonstrate incompetence at best, or lying opportunist, deceitful to the Republic and our people probably the utmost.

Are we in the United States *sovereign* individuals? This with most absolute certainly. I believe this is true, as we are according to the U.S. Constitution. The purpose of this discourse is to investigate and expose the principles of not only what it means to be sovereign, but of sovereignty in general and whether the U.S. Constitution actually guarantees the individual sovereign status. This discourse will touch on the differences between our republicanism, democracy form of government and the actual make-up of the United States with regard to the U.S. Constitution as well as the beliefs of our *founding fathers*.

What is sovereignty? Black's Law Dictionary 2nd Ed. defines sovereignty, "The possession of sovereign power; supreme political authority; paramount control of the constitution and frame of government and its administration; the self-sufficient source of political power, from which all specific political powers are originated." By definition, sovereignty gives the ownership of power; and the ultimate political power to determine; preeminent direction over the make-up and structure of not only the government, but the administration of the government as well; the provision for one to supply for his own needs, without external assistance; and the source of our ability to act with regard to politics. This as all politicians derive their just power from the consent of the governed.

We, the people are the rightful masters of both Congress, the courts, and the All Administrations, not to overthrow the Constitution, but to overthrow those men who have perverted the Constitution.

Article IV, Section 4 of the U.S. Constitution states, "The United States shall guarantee to every State in this Union a Republican Form of Government." Article VI, Clause 2 states, "This Constitution, and the Laws of the United States which shall be made in Pursuance thereof...under the Authority of the United States, shall be the supreme Law of the Land". As unequivocally stated in the U.S. Constitution, the sovereign power which is vested in the people through Republicanism is *guaranteed* by the supreme Law of the Land, the Constitution of the United States. There can be no doubt, our forefathers, believed in the sovereign individual or the U.S. Constitution would clearly state otherwise, we the people of the United States are a democracy? Yet nowhere within the U.S. Constitution is the word democracy even mentioned. Therefore the Constitution is not an instrument for the government to restrain the people, it is an instrument for the people to restrain government. Patrick Henryi[v]

All words in the following proceedings not in italics are mine, all other individual's words are in italics.

Plaintiff's Accusation, First Challenge

Anti-Injunction Act

The Anti-Injunction Act has thus been constructed as a penalty, not as a tax as implied by Chief Justice Roberts, also Justices Ginsburg, Breyer, Sotomayor, and Kagan. This was clarified, since it was clearly stated as a penalty and not a tax, then under the Anti- Injunction Act and because the individual mandate of Affordable Care Act labeled and argued by the government it was noted a penalty, hence one must assume it was a penalty. The Anti-Injunction Act imposes a pay first, litigate later rule that is central to Federal tax, what Federal tax was assessed and collected. The Act applies to essentially every tax penalty, again what tax is penalized, in the Internal Revenue Code at 5000A. There is no reason to think that Congress made a special exception for the penalty imposed by section 5000A. On the contrary, there are but three reasons to conclude that the Anti-Injunction Act applies here.

First, Congress directed that the section 5000A penalty shall be assessed and collected in the same manner as taxes, this statement is untrue. Second, Congress provided that penalties are added to taxes for assessment and purposes. This statement is improper in terms thus on the face thereof. This should read taxes are penalized for failure to properly pay taxes. Thirdly, section 5000A penalty clauses bear the key *indicia* of a tax. The word indicia means, (indications of the existence of a given fact) nowhere in 5000A could one indeed suggest a given fact to a key of a tax.

The other four Justices, Scalia, Kennedy, Thomas and Alito also agreed but for other reasons. *As the mandate was not a tax in the first place, plus having no bearing whatsoever on the label.*

In the government's arguments, no less then eighteen (18) times, stating that it was a penalty in fact NOT a tax. Yet John Roberts continued to declare it a tax overriding the government's own position that it was a penalty and NOT a tax. As a citizen I find this quite incomprehensible and perplexing. What new tax has he created and from what source, moreover what label has he placed upon the same. However, he was asked concerning the tax in this regard, conversely he chose not answering these pertinent questions to the court.

Quote of Justice Roberts *"The Affordable Care Act requires that an applicable individual* (NOTE failing to define applicable individual) *failure to maintain essential coverage as a requirement may be penalized, this may reasonably be characterized as a tax. Therefore it is not my role to forbid it, or pass upon its wisdom or fairness."* Furthermore, John Roberts stated it was the courts duty for finding ways to support the law, affirming:
"Though this court will often strain to construe legislation so as to save it against Constitutional attack". I find his assertion totally inexplicable.

We find his statement to be untrue and incorrect, rather it's the duty of the court to examine the law, considering how the law may fit after reading the same statute. Then how would this particular statute be in accord with the characteristics within the framework of the Constitution, being fundamental and complete? The framers were of the intent that the Constitution would be the obstacle to reign in wild and runaway legislatures. It's the framework of our Constitution, thus meant to be held to the highest of laws in our republic. They the legislators are required to protect and uphold the Constitution by their oath or affirmation into office.

Justices dissenting, Justice Scalia, Kennedy, Thomas, Alito. The dissent takes issue with what it views as a jurisprudential novelty: They submitted, *"independently authorized suggests the existence of a creature never hitherto seen in the United States Reports: A penalty for Constitutional purposes that is also a tax for Constitutional purposes. In all our cases the two are mutually exclusive"*. Congress cannot pass something that is both a tax and a penalty, and the government cannot plead that it be considered as such because, as the dissent writes, *"the provision challenged under the Constitution is either a penalty or else a tax"*, quoted Justice Scalia.

The dissent continues...

Of course in many cases what was a regulatory mandate enforced by a penalty, could have been imposed as a tax upon permissible action; or what was imposed as a tax upon permissible action could have been a regulatory mandate enforced by a penalty. But we know of no case, and the Government cites none, in which the imposition was, for Constitutional purposes, both. Thank you gentlemen. If I may be so presumptuous I would like to engender a thought with regards to the tax.

The Anti-Injunction act, as the act restrains one from executing an injunction against the Internal Revenue Service until April of 2015,

How then does the court achieve its goal of passing judgment on any of the other issues, getting past the Anti- Injunction Act. It seems the Anti- Injunction act is dangling in space.

Let us explore the words of admonition by one Thomas Jefferson and I quote those words for the court, as they seem to have forgotten or don't care as long as the body politic has been served, this factual unembellished statement bears repeating.

"On every Question of the Construction let us carry ourselves back to the time when the Constitution was adopted, recollect the spirit manifested in the debates and instead of trying what meaning may be squeezed out of the text, or invented against it, conform to the probable one in which it was passed".

Again I ask if the mandate is a tax rather than a penalty. How then would the Anti-Injunction Act be applied? This more than ever begs the question, how does the Supreme Court apply an unknown, unanswered mandate to an unanswered Anti-Injunction act. For myself, the whole question of the Affordable Care Act, which it is not, is rather merely a hoax. Had these needs been remanded to the states as the 9th and 10th amendments requires, since the individual states are far more equipped for best understanding. Therefore able to meet the needs of their constituents. Hence by amending the Affordable Care Act, eliminating the I.R.S., what a cost saving. The funds which the President has stolen (716 billion), from the existing Medicare fund plus the I.R.S expenditure, plus the cost of the additional Medicaid Act, however yet to be argued by the court. One could assume the accumulative funds (trillions of dollars) divided equally amongst the fifty states (not fifty-seven as the President Obama erroneously imagines), according to their population. I included the below section of the arguments in the Supreme Court to show how capricious and whimsical their actions regarding time spent over the Anti-Injunction Act.

Then it's your money their spending, I ask why would the court concern themselves, plus the outcome being without merit on the face of it. Although standing between the Supreme Court and a politically charged decision upholding or striking down a mandate. In like manner, such as in the law with regards to the reconstruction era. The Tax Anti-Injunction Act, which: *forbids lawsuits filed for the purpose of restraining the assessment or collection of any tax until after that tax has been paid.*

The penalty is a tax because it will be paid at the same time as one's tax return. This statement is again without merit on its face, yet fantastic for childish thinking, as the tax is supposedly calculated on a monthly basis.

The court: *The Tax Anti-Injunction Act would not prevail, if read though the act were a penalty.*

Confusion amongst the ranks?

The questions focused on how to wiggle out of the law's flat ban on tax-restraining lawsuits and how to avoid the conclusion that the mandate's penalty is, in fact, *a* tax.

This was by no means a simple task.

Long (attorney for the state) told the justices that Congress said the *"penalty shall be assessed and collected in the same manner as taxes,"* but Justice Antonin Scalia suggested that courts owed no deference to that determination because, he said, *"it was directed solely to the Treasury Department"*. Justice Ruth Bader Ginsburg contrasted the Anti- Injunction Act's *"no suit ... shall be maintained"* language with that of a sister statute that expressly bans *"courts of the United States from delaying certain proceedings"*. This contrast, she contended, *makes the Anti-Injunction Act unconstitutional.* Suitor directed in contrast to court-directed. *Never mind the rest of the statute, which reads, in any court by any person.*

Then Justice Samuel Alito, for his part, implied that several past cases set the precedent that the *"Congress is not denominating it as a tax; it's denominating it as a penalty,"* Sotomayor said "the penalty is *not_attached to a tax,"* Justice Breyer states. *"It is attached to the health care requirement,"*

But Sotomayor asked, *"What's the parade of horribles, that would occur if the Anti-Injunction Act were something that the government could assume appropriate at its own discretion"?*

Long an "attorney" was not able to give a sufficient answer, so Scalia answered for him.

"I will answer for him, if it were the government discretion, deciding how to apply the Anti-Injunction Act, where would it end". We the people could be forced into buying anything or compulsory acting as we were told, NO FREEWILL.

"What'*s going to happen is, you are going to have an intelligent federal court deciding whether you are going to make an exception".* Scalia questioned.

With the high court apparently unanimously arrayed against the lawyer they had appointed to argue before them, Solicitor General Donald Verrilli and the challengers' lawyer, Gregory Katas, were freed to tell the Justices how to get past the Anti-Injunction Act.

Verrilli's main problem was getting past his own hair-splitting attempt to define "tax" to the government's benefit. The penalty is a tax for Constitutional purposes, he argued. Now looking ahead to the intricacies of Tuesday's debate.

Nevertheless, he said, *it is not a tax under the Internal Revenue Code, which is what matters for the Anti-Injunction Act analysis.*

Verrilli was asked *"today you are arguing that the penalty is not a tax,"* Justice Alito said. *"Tomorrow you are going to be back and you will be arguing that the penalty is a tax".*

Question, *"Has the Court ever held that something that is a tax for purposes of the taxing power under the Constitution is not a tax under the Anti-Injunction Act?"* Alito asked.

Verrilli said no. A side note: Thomas Jefferson believed members of the Supreme Court ought to be elected as others serving in our Republic and for a term, not for life. *"Furthermore, they need to remember from whence our Republic began, then* laws written by our legislators, today more than ever, after Nancy Pelosi's wild

statement, *"pass it so you can read what's in it, away from the fog of controversy"*. This is not such a noble idea Justice Roberts, pass the law and then YOU find a way to uphold it.
A categorization of the details in such a manner as to satisfy the legislators. What about the fact that you, nor the legislators have read this bill and how it might affect the People and our Republic. Some of the court and the Chief Justice in particular, have little regard for the American citizen, being those which employs them.

In order to clarify the long winded, rhetorical exchange of dialogue, of which they continued to argue with regards to the Anti- Injunction Act. An inordinate portion of their time arguing whether it was a penalty or tax, subsequently prior to determining which was the appropriate choice, the government withdrew their argument. Now I am obliged to *undertake for which they were hired, applying the Constitution to all laws consistently and equally"*. These are the thoughts of a very wise man and the result of a wise man's thinking.

These thoughts should be the basis for any court to discern, any and all comments on this issue, as this is a prime example of government in action, **"what fools we mortals be"**!

The **Anti-Injunction Act**, (chapter. 22 of the Acts for the 2nd United States Congress, 2nd Session, **1 Stat. 333, 28 U.S.C. § 2283),** is a United States federal statute that prohibits any federal court from issuing an injunction against proceedings in any state court, except within three specifically defined exceptions. The Act was enacted on March 2, 1793 as Section 5 of the Judiciary Act of 1793, to alleviate states' fears of federal power. Take note of their opinion.

A court of the United States may not grant an injunction to stay proceedings in a state court except as expressly authorized by **one**, Act of Congress, **two**, where necessary in aid of its jurisdiction, or **three** to protect or effectuate its judgments.

The "tax Anti-Injunction Act" was originally enacted as **Pub L. 39-169, 14 Stat 475, section 7421(a)** of the Internal Revenue Code of 1954 (now the 1986 Code).

Though his was a contradiction in terms, Justice Roberts prevailed and the word penalty was injected as he stated *"the word penalty must apply for Constitutional purpose"*. Thus the Chief Justice, has the Supreme court playing with words as if they have no explicit or significance of meaning in his statement *"Though this court will often strain to construe legislation so as to save it against Constitutional attack"*. Think of what Justice John Roberts mind is contemplating, when he stated it must read PENALTY in the Anti-Injunction Act for Constitutional purpose. Then has the gall to suggest, this court will often strain to construe legislation so as to save it against Constitutional attack. One, consider this ideology, an incredible indication of Chief Justice Roberts' perception of the Constitution, then too his scheme of legal concepts designed and explained by precise words. This is a ludicrous suggestion and preposterous thinking. As a citizen I am appalled, outraged and insulted by his interpretations of our Constitution relevant to laws enacted by congresses since congress is beholding to the Constitution. Justice Roberts believes incorrectly so, to any extent that one is able to observe his willingness to twist words and case law, into his role as Chief Justice, rather than law needing to align itself with the Constitution, he states the Constitution must align itself with the law. To my view better to my acquaintance with the Constitution, I believe he's either totally incompetent, a liar, perhaps in all, probability both.

Plaintiff's Accusation, Second Challenge

Taxing power clause, a mandate of the Affordable Care Act. Chief Justice John Roberts' case law, an attempt to support his delusions.

Reflecting on the time spent arguing the anti-injunction act, there has been an overabundance of bloviating, quite a fiasco which truly had little if any application to the Affordable Care Act. Regardless, I will move ahead with my accusations, beginning with meaning of words, as each have some particular meaning. Then expectantly, I hope to bring some of Chief Justice John Roberts basic case law to assess his thinking, if possible or at least evaluate them. Therefore, studying and considering the words of the court, which I have examined in section 5000A (a) of the Internal Revenue Service while they have utilized words which they intentionally distorted and misused. This to describe whom they believe came under the Affordable Care Act... Example: *"an applicable individual"*. Perhaps repeating myself from the previous accusation, if so, I have decided to ensure a result, I proceed. Noah Webster defines applicable a*s an adj. "that which can be applied, or fit to be appropriately applicable"*. Applicable being the mechanism which gives capability for an applicant to apply. Then again we find Noah Webster defines applicant as: *one who applies or makes a request, a petitioner.* While individual: *as an adj. or noun not divisible, or separable. 2. Existing as separate things, or persons.*

I find the operational use of these words confusing and within the realm of miscalculation. The choice of the word person would have come about honest and enough. Furthermore, if one is attempting to speak honestly, then they would have used the proper word, **Applicant,** stating at its root rationale. As in, I wish to apply for work as a painter, thus becoming an **applicant** by choice. Of course this was not the courts objective, perverting and faking the meaning, their intended distortion.

 As for any intent to force an **applicant** when it's clearly a matter of choice, is another example of the government's problems with the truth. Furthermore the issue is beyond and outside the purview and determination of this court. Below are but a few of Justice Roberts's case laws used to support his position. I have read and copied many other texts of his case law, (available to you upon request) but all are not included in my arguments, as they would not contribute further to the lack of validity to his arguments, nor would enhance mine, only increase the size of an already oversized text,

 Justice Roberts words "we must if fairly possible" in which he used **Crowell vs. Benson**, [285 U.S. 22, 62} (1932) as an example of his assessment in 5000A IRS 1986 code. Rather this case concerning damages to person operating in U.S. navigable waters, manipulating them to corroborate his contentions. In truth this case was better served under the authority of Admiralty courts, as it was so stated within the body of that transcript.

The following paragraphs of **Crowell vs. Benson 285 U.S.** are but a brief portion of this case, over twenty pages of which I found not one rational reason to further exploit.

Justice Roberts own position remained, as he was willing to convolute his own words during the Affordable Care Act case.

The administrative bodies in the cases referred to by the Court, on the contrary, are in no sense fact-gathering [285 U.S. 22, 89] or fact-finding tribunals of first instance. They are tribunals of final resort within the scope of their authority. Their concern is with matters ordinarily outside of judicial competence. The deportation of aliens, the enforcement of military discipline, the granting of land patents, and the use of the mails-matters which are within the power of Congress to commit to conclusive executive determination.

In virtue of its power to alter or revise the maritime law, Congress may provide that, where employees in maritime employment are disabled or die from accidental injuries arising out of or in the course of their employment upon the navigable waters of the United States

As I stated previously, a case for the Maritime Court or Court of last resort.

Compare Ex parte **Bakelite Corporation, 279 U.S. 438, 451, 49 S. Ct. 411**. Their procedure may be summary and frequently remains. With respect to them, the function of the courts is not one of review but essentially of control,-the function of keeping them within their statutory authority. **[285 U.S. 22, 90]** No method of judicial review of the administrative action had been provided by Congress in any of the cases cited; and the question of the power to confine review to the administrative record accordingly did not arise. In each case, the Court held that, *if the administrative officer had acted outside his authority, the unwritten law supplied a remedy, and that relief could be had, according to the nature of the case, on bill in equity or habeas corpus.* **[285 U.S. 22, 91]**

Without exception I found no reference to the idea of exchanging one word for another, of any convolution of words, anywhere. As a matter of these issues pertaining to The Affordable Care Act, the facts stand in these cases, are deprived of support in case law or remedy by federal courts or any Tribunal or the Court of final resort. Justice Roberts words of Tax or Penalty were without use a as analogous, similar words.

The question decided in each case was that Congress should not be taken, in the absence of specific provision, to have intended to subject the person to the uncontrolled action of a public administrative officer. See American School of **Magnetic Healing v. MacNulty, 187 U.S. 94, 110 23 S. Ct. 33.** No comparable issue is presented here.

The statement below which is pertinent to this case, was part of the dissenting statement.

Justices, Brandeis, Stone and Roberts (not the current Justice Roberts*). My evaluation of the affirmative, within the particulars subject to those*

questions emanating from this case. I find no suggestion of referring to words not made available, somewhere within the essence, or the body of either of these case.

Crowell vs Benson, *285 U. S. 22, 62(1932).*   As has been exhibited and explained, "**Every single reasonable construction must be resorted to, in order to save a statue from unconstitutional action**". For myself unconstitutional and Constitutional are quite the opposite, inverse in thought. The socialist idea is revealed by Chief Justice John Roberts attempt at expanding and convoluting these two words.

No worthy reason is suggested when all the evidence which Benson presented to the District Court in this cause could not have been presented before the deputy commissioner; nor why he should have permitted to present his case provisionally, before the administrative tribunal and then to retry it in the District Court upon additional evidence theretofore withheld. Permitting him to do so violates the salutary principle that administrative remedies must first be exhausted, before resorting to the court, to imposes an unnecessary and burdensome expense upon the other party and cripples the effective administration of the act. (This is part of the Anti-Injunction Act). Which was settled earlier in The Anti-Injunction Act debacle.

Under the prevailing practice, by which the Judicial review has been confined to questions of law, the proceedings before the deputy commissioners, **[285 U.S. 22, 94]** have proven for the most part, rather relatively few cases have reached the courts. To permit a contest, *de novo (trying a matter anew), as if no decision had been rendered in the District Court of an issue tried, or tried before the deputy commissioner will, I fear, gravely hamper the effectiveness of the administration of the act itself.*

The prestige of the deputy commissioner will necessarily be lessened by the opportunity of again litigating facts in the courts. The number of controverted cases may be largely increased. Persistence in controversy will be encouraged, since this idea increases the requirement and of the involvement and interest or activity of upsurge in lawyers. And since the advantage of prolonged litigation lies with the party able to bear heavy expenses, the purpose of the act will be in part defeated. [285 U.S. 22, 95]. In my opinion the judgment of the Circuit Court of Appeal should be reversed and the case remanded to the District Court. Sitting as a court of equity, for consideration and decision upon the record made before the deputy commissioner. Regardless no substance for an avenue of concern, may judge reason for our issue.

Mr. Justice STONE and Mr. Justice ROBERTS (past) joined in this opinion. After having read this case, it was my consensus, it occurred singularly and intended to facilitate another issue entirely, as it had insignificant issue with the question of these words, in fact none, **penalty** or **taxes.** Nor did there exist any mention of taxes on any issue, nor in the least by supplementary means.

Although I did find this relevant decision in the body of **"Crowell vs. Benson".** The contention based upon the judicial power of the United States, as extended 'to all Cases of **Admiralty [285 U.S. 22, 49]** and maritime Jurisdiction' (Constitution Art. 3), presents a distinct but separate question concerning this matter.

In the reading of these cases used in support of the A.C.A. case. I found nowhere were the words penalty and tax used interchangeably, in fact the word tax was not mentioned, nor any words used inter-changeable.

In Murray's **Lessee v. Hoboken Land & Improvement Company, 18 How. 272, 284,** this Court, speaking through Justice Curtis, said: *"To avoid misconstruction upon so grave a subject, we think it proper to state that we do not consider congress can either withdraw from Judicial cognizance any matter which, from its nature is the subject of a suit at the common law, or in equity, or admiralty. Nor, on the other hand, can it bring under the judicial power a matter which, from its nature, is not a subject for judicial determination".*

Chief Justice Roberts in his affirmative decision used Justice Ginsburg's statement *"The Federal Government does not have the power to order people to buy health insurance. Section 5000Aa of the Internal Revenue Code, would therefore be unconstitutional if read as a command."* Rather Justice Ginsburg misread and or misstated these words when she said, *"Federal Government does have the power to impose a tax on those without health insurance. Section 5000Aa is therefore constitutional, because it can reasonably be read as a tax".* Nowhere is tax mentioned, as I am sure section 5000Aa is attempting to determine those who, each month shall be required to be covered by minimum essential coverage, for myself it's quite yet an undetermined amount. Reading on, those failing will be **penalized** each month. If coerced by a tax to purchase insurance, or failure to do so, it remains unconstitutional.

Peculiar that the code reads *"will be penalized each month"*, noting the word penalized and without an undetermined amount.

I have judiciously read 5000Aa to the extreme. This section reads... **Requirement** to maintain minimum essential coverage.

An applicable individual **shall**…now the words require and shall: **Webster's Require**, *"is to ask or insist by right or authority, to order or command."* **Shall, "**to *be required, in the mandatory sense used in courts."*

Black's Law dictionary, *"it means to command"* and **require** is used similarly. It fails to occur or subsist within our Constitution, apart from government's duty with respect toward the citizen? This modest fact, basically does not exist, rather it applies to elected persons to whom serve in and all political positions, all at the discretion of the people.

In this case I raise and am obliged to explain the misuse of these two very important words, applicable and individual, now I discover myself in a similar situation, exposing their attempt to confuse the issue with the words, require and shall. However, both these words indicate a command to an **applicant,** one without choice, a simple yea or nay to purchase or not, health care insurance. Please remember this is not about health care, but insurance. I care not how Justice Roberts states or of how **he** thinks it may be similar to, workable or may be read, but rather what it states in black and white, consistent and appropriately part of the English language. It exist so, and is clearly written as a command, unless by chance he is ignorant of the truths, failing our republic's history and the use of the English language. Again we should examine and also consider being enlightened by Thomas Jefferson pertaining to our Constitution related to such a situation, *"not to invent against it, conform to the probable one in which it was passed"*

In all six dictionaries I have, three Black's law Dictionary and three of Webster's dating back to 1828, I find all six affirm, as to the words require and shall to mean a command. In the face of all these words Chief Justice John Roberts remains akin "the king lacks intellect".

Other cases: Liberty University, Inc. et al v. Geithner et al Western District of Virginia **Plaintiffs:**
Liberty University, Inc., and the individual **Defendants:** Timothy Geithner, Kathleen Sibelius, Hilda Solis, Eric Holder

Judge: Norman K. Moon, Referred to: Magistrate Judge Michael F. Urbanski

Case number: *6: 10-c v- 00015*

Details: Plaintiffs' case is similar to Virginia v. Sibelius, challenging the Patient Protection and Affordable Care Act based on Virginia law. The Plaintiffs objection to the use of public funds for abortions, and also raised objections on First Amendment grounds, including an assertion that PPACA expresses a preference for one religion over others. Finally, the Complaint claims that PPACA violates the guarantee of a Republican form of government.

Status: An Amended Complaint was filed July 30. The Defendants had filed a Motion to dismiss the case. A hearing on the Motion to Dismiss occurred on October 22. On November 30, the Court denied the Defendants' Motion to Dismiss. On December 1, Plaintiffs filed for appeal.

On May 10, 2011, a three-judge panel from the Fourth Circuit Court of Appeals heard oral arguments in this case. The panel was comprised of two Obama-appointees and one Clinton-appointee. On September 8, 2011, the Fourth Circuit panel dismissed the case. They found that the individual mandate was a tax (the first court to do so), and because of the Anti-Injunction Act, plaintiffs cannot challenge it in court until it is collected (in 2015).

This case *3:10-cv.-00188-HEH*, the state of Virginia is attempting to exercise their right of sovereignty, by way of the

Ninth and Tenth amendments. The court merely brushed it aside. Furthermore, the state of Virginia passed a law protecting its citizens from monstrous federal action, stating: *"No resident of this Commonwealth, regardless of whether he has or is eligible for health insurance coverage under any policy or program provided by or through his employer, or a plan sponsored by the Commonwealth or the federal government, shall be required to obtain or maintain a policy of individual insurance coverage. No provision of this title shall render residents of this Commonwealth liable for any penalty, assessment, fee, or fine as a result of his failure to procure or obtain health insurance coverage". "If the citizens of the United States should not be free and happy, the fault will be entirely their own."* George Washington

Again I am persuaded against the Justice stating that **perans patriae,** as We the People rule, hopefully we recuperate our ailing, lying federal government. I ask, is our parental government supreme, or are the individual people the supreme leaders of this our republic. These Latin words **perans patriae** may be found in any law dictionary, but you may already know them. I found in another court challenging approximately the same action.

Liberty University vs. Timothy Geithner, Kathleen Sibelius and Eric Holder. In my opinion both of these cases for the plaintiffs, were wisely and correctly presented, nevertheless they were distressingly and disturbingly dismissed One of the Justices stated a Congressional position on the Affordable Care Act was to force (unconstitutional) the states to adopt federal

standards and mandates, or they would forfeit *"or lose their sovereignty"*. How? This suggestion is without merit and unconstitutional. Following this order to force, they lose, failing to proceed according to Ninth and Tenth amendments, begets the same loss to the states and their people. Thus the Ninth and Tenth amendments would have become no longer valid, or acknowledged by the national government. His statement was outrageous and without thought or substance.

This is how Germany began in the early nineteen thirties, the people were beholding to the government, *perans patriae,* is the court suggesting this as well, similarly. Europe was already on the road to fascism, from their own governments, no longer will be able to grant them the nanny state of which they had become accustom, of which we ourselves, may soon witness. Furthermore Virginia argued; **US 213,224,116S, Ct.2106, 2112**   On the other hand, a penalty imports the notion of punishment for an unlawful act or omission, the two words Tax vs. Penalty, are not interchangeable and if exaction is clearly a penalty it cannot be converted into a tax by the simple expedients of calling it such.

United States vs. La Franca 282 U.S. 568,51S Ct. 278,280, (1931).

Also the Commonwealth points out that elsewhere in the act, Congress specifically described levies as taxes, such as section **9001,9004, 9015, 9017, S. Ct. 449, 450 (1922).** To amplify its point, the Commonwealth focuses the Court's attention on a series of cases in which the Supreme Court struck down certain "regulatory taxes" as an unconstitutional encroachment on the State's power of regulation under the Tenth Amendment.

See Butler, 297 U.S. at 68, 56 S. Ct. at 320. Linder v. United States, 268 U.S. 5, 1718, 45 S. Ct. 446, 449 (1925); Child Labor Tax Case, 259 U.S. at 35, 42 S. Ct. at 451. In commenting on the limitations on the power of Congress to levy taxes to promote the general welfare, the Court in Butler noted that, *"despite the breadth of the legislative discretion, our duty to hear and to render judgment remains. If the statute plainly violates the stated principle of the Constitution, we must so declare."_Butler, 297*

U.S. at 67, 56 S. Ct. at 320; also Kahriger, 345 U.S. at 29, 73 S. Ct. at 513."

Again the commonwealth argued although the Commonwealth concedes that the power of Congress to tax exceeds its ability to regulate under the Commerce Clause, it is not without limitation. *"The law is that Congress can tax under its taxing power that which it can't regulate, but it can't regulate through taxation that which it cannot otherwise regulate."* **(Tr. 81:18-21, July 1, 2010)** *citing.*

Bailey v Drexel Furniture Co. (Child Labor Tax Case), 259 U.S. 20, 37, 42.

Thus by comparison, the Commonwealth argues that the Minimum Essential Coverage Provision not only invokes rights reserved to the states, but also seeks to compel activity beyond the reach of Congress. As discussed above, the division of responsibility for regulating insurance between the Commonwealth and the federal government, to the extent relevant, is yet to be adequately staked out in this case. In addition it is my obligation to note in this case, all references to case law, in this particular case by the government are after 1913. In my opinion this fact is so clearly evident and predictable, as the income tax law (*the 16 th Amendment* plus the Federal Reserve all began in 1913). Think about this incident, chance, I think not, the timing was meant to promote criminal engagements against the people of our republic. Reading these cases in their entirety, one finds the government in collusion with itself (congress and the courts), as I believe both are without merit on the very face of their arguments. It is my desire to address the constitutional issues involved in the above cases. I am in the condition of disbelief, as one finds the courts have positioned themselves somewhere between fiction and lies, quite impossible to discover a bit of integrity. This paragraph is an expression of my opinion and not necessarily fact but probably true, nonetheless

I have read and reread the perpetuity in these cases, using their words to advance my conclusion, these are the Liberty University and Virginia cases.

In a widespread action they merely swept the plaintiffs evidence away, thus deprived of any consideration. In reality they simply destroyed both the 9th and 10th Amendments of our Constitution. Plus among other issues, such as threating to suffer the loss of their soveriegnty.

How could anyone explain the loss of a state's soveriegnty, when as each state has their own constitution which demands they remain as sovereign states? It's called Judicial Deference and is starved of law, only the dogma of the Justices themselves.

WE WILL FURTHER ADDRESS SOME OF THE ISSUES IN THE FOLLOWING SECTION BY SHOWING HOW FAR CHIEF JUSTICE JOHN ROBERTS WILL REACH, WITH DECEPTION AND INACCURACIES IN HIS REPRESENTATIONS THIS IN ORDER TO PROPAGANDIZE HIS AGENDA, JOHN ROBERTS SUGGEST HIS INTERPRETATION FOUND IN THE FOLLOWING SECTIONS OF THE IRS CODE. U.S. CODE › TITLE 26 › SUBTITLE D › CHAPTER 48 › § 5000A CURRENT THROUGH PUB. L. 114-38. U.S. CODE › TITLE 26 › SUBTITLE D › CHAPTER 48 › § 5000A READS: REQUIREMENT TO MAINTAIN MINIMUM ESSENTIAL COVERAGE, SEE 5000A (A)

Plaintiff's Accusation Third Challenge

Let us look at 5000 A (a) and exactly how it reads:

To maintain minimum essential coverage - *An applicable individual shall maintain for each month, beginning after 2013 ensure that the individual, and any dependent of the individual who is an applicable individual, is covered under minimum essential coverage for such.*

 The obvious initial question remains , how does one deal with the concept of a dependent becoming an "applicable individual" when an applicable individual has hitherto explained as an individual choosing to apply.

 I find in Justice Roberts determination of 5000Aa and my analyses of same, progressed into an adversarial struggle, John Roberts shapes his attempt by a brazen exploitation of our Constitution and the IRS code. Furthermore, Chief Justice Roberts, implies **U.S. Code › Title 26 › Subtitle D › Chapter 48 › § 5000A (a), A (b), A(c)** one must accept his indulgence in deception as seen here (*if one should reasonably read the section 5000A, then the following sections 5000Aa, Ab and Ac could if reasonably read, as tax*). It appears to me there is not one scintilla of truth in his statement, let's read it again (*if one should reasonably read the section 5000A, then the following sections 5000Aa, Ab and Ac could if reasonably read as tax*) if one is lacking the ability to read and comprehend English, or as he or she requires help understanding English. Then they should seek that help grasping this phrase. These words are interjected by John Roberts and they are never found in 5000A or 5000Aa nor Sec.

5000Ab and 5000Ac as John Roberts realized well he was lying, creating the illusion they too may be construed to mean tax, when 5000A has not a shred of evidence of a tax, or the suggestion of same. His approval therefore is simply a lie, nothing else.

I have taken this opportunity and counted the times the word **penalty** is interjected, thus ten times and never once **Tax**. This in the first portion of 5000A, 5000Aa and 5000Ab, (1), (2), (3) 3(a)(b) B and 5000 Ac, all this one half page, the penalty page. If all tax, are as provided for in sec. 8 of Article One of our Constitution, *"excises shall be uniform throughout the United States"*, how then will it be applied at a sliding scale and fined monthly as detailed in 5000Ac,c)(1thru 3)including sub, sub sections. So like some magician's misdirection, now you see it now you are confused. Please check my statements in the 1986 IRS code, this as well as Blacks Law found in your library.

This with voluminous dissertation, words saying nothing all the while, upon examination never observing the word tax, finding only penalty. Reading on to the second page as part of 5000Ac, we observe the scale for which I just mentioned, penalties not taxes outlined on the previous page and all penalties applied as stated. Then page 3- 5000Ad gives an explanation to a summary of those who may be exempt, if not excluded by an amendment. These are primarily religious exemptions, under specific situations stipulated in 501C3 of the tax code, where we Christians lost our right to speak out for or against the government. This provision was tacked to an important piece of legislation, nevertheless Christanty is being brought under attack more so today.

Then fourth page - 5000Ae, one finds fourteen sub- and sub-subsections, of which I refrained from lettering. Required some contributions, specials rules related to employees, indexing

Members of Indian Tribes and Tax payers below the taxing threshold, plus Hardships, Section 5000Af.

Page 5 defines the threshold for minimum coverage. Reframing with regards and alluding to or attempting to explain at this time, all 23 subsections and sub-sub-sections one will encounter, nor defining these sections will neither add nor diminish or assist in destroying the individual mandate, check this for yourself.

Section 5000Ag page 6 covers "Indoor Tanning Services", while using the word penalty four additional times, while the word tax is non-existent. On page 6 we encounter 5000B, Ba, Bb, Bc, plus as always amendments.

This section covers "Elective cosmetic medical procedures." It truly matters not, since 5000Aa was distorted and misrepresented by Justice Roberts. Don't you find it strange as I have, to discover the I.R.S. code covered the entire Affordable Health Care Act in six pages, while Congress required twenty seven hundred plus pages attempting to explain their own thinking with regards to their own words in their legislation, aren't we missing something at this point. The full title of this act "Patient Protection and Affordable Care Act and **other things**". Question, what other things? As I read and reread this section of the Affordable Care Act, one will find taxes and regulations, controled by non-elected persons and therefore highly injurious to this issue, finding these persons are not in the medical field and multiple interjections of various types, without answers.

Therefore, this past March 2014, the Obama administration issued its latest "fix" to the troubled roll out of the Affordable Care Act. The Center for Medicare & Medicaid Services issued a guidance that permits federal funds to go to insurers and insured involved in sale of an individual health insurance outside of either a federally established or state established Exchange. The premise of the guidance is that, in certain states such as Maryland, Massachusetts,

Hawaii and Oregon, the complete dysfunctional use of the websites, were intended to determine eligibility for Obamacare subsidies may have led people to enroll in policies off the Exchanges.

These purchasers, the guidance directs, those should be treated identically, as if the state Exchanges had made a timely determination and the individuals had enrolled in an Exchange policy though they had not. Further depressing, is the House members and Senators, had never read this 2700 page boondoggle "work of little or no value". Remember our congresswoman from San Francisco statement, "But we have to pass the bill so you can find out what is in it". Now unfortunately, we have come to discover what's in the bill which Nancy Pelosi insisted we pass, so it should become known to all Americans. Even in a democracy, which we are not, rather sounds quite similar to a dictatorship, certainly not a Republic.

Plaintiff's Accusation Fourth Challenge

Confusion as to the meaning of our Constitution

While I may have addressed these arguments aggressively, I obtain no comfort or pleasure in doing so, in fact it grieves me that we have allowed our government to become so corrupt, on the good side, lazy, inept and bungling. Of course not all, rather many examples the U.S. Supreme Court of which we are challenging at this time. Again an example, when the court was arguing the Anti-injunction Act, it was determined the word penalty would remain as it was correct and Constitutional, though they argued for some hours, finally Chief Justice John Roberts acknowledged changing penalty to tax would be unconstitutional. Then he simply grabbed a breath and without flinching said (*if one should reasonable read the section 5000A, then the following sections 5000Aa, Ab and Ac could, if reasonably read, as tax*) thus it became so. Now we have moved to the subject of the Affordable Care Act from the Anti-Injunction Act. The exchanging of these words have then become Constitutional. Now must we commit to the proposition defined by the court, concluding hereafter the words penalty and tax are synonyms, I expect not.

Justice Roberts ... *"The Federal Government does not have the power to order people to buy health insurance. Section 5000A (of THE INTERNAL REVENUE SERVICE) would therefore be unconstitutional if read as a command."* Previously I stated, due to Webster's definition of the word *"**requirement** found it to mean a **command**, especially in the legal utilization, or application, as to insist, a command by authority"*. It appears our Chief Justice is incapable of knowing or grasping the meaning of our American English language, as stated earlier. The answer appears in the negative indeed. Furthermore, he makes claims to magic words or labels, which should not disable an otherwise Constitutional levy. However he goes on *"the Federal Government does have the power to impose a tax on those without health insurance. Section 5000a is therefore Constitutional, because it can be reasonably read as a tax"*. This is his opinion, so the question remains where, anywhere has he been given the authority, or granted the power to exchange, convert, or magically insert the word tax in place of the written word? However let's read Mr. Webster opinion.

Tax: A rate or sum of money assessed on the person or property of a citizen by government for the use of the nation to defray its expenses. **Penalty**: *The suffering in person or property which by law or judicial decision to the commission of a crime, or trespass are inflicted upon the person subsist, as usually penalties are imprisonment, hard labor or death. Then for the non-compliance of an agreement: the penalty of a bond.* To what agreement is Justice John Roberts referring, I suggest again he has conjured something from out of thin air, crafting or creating something by magical means. It behooves the court to make clear the implication, significance and connotation of an imaginary, or fictitious contract one enters into with the government. Thus referring to the words shall and requirement, both meaning a command especially in a court of law. Expecting no answer I will respond honestly, they are deprived of any, lacking in the necessary phrasing by the Congress, they, Congress would have finished and gone down in flames. Furthermore, in my judgment Justice Roberts not only willfully confers a new definition, (none written), to **requirement**, but insist on our cooperation to presume his argument over Noah Webster's is correct. Additionally, Justice Roberts comes to the conclusion that penalty and tax are synonymous words, since they are synonymous therefore could be read as being the same, thus we must assume he maintains the mantel of Chief Justice of ultimate authority and critic of Noah Webster's American English dictionary and others, plus Black's Law Dictionary.

 Hence we find Black's law definition *"The rule by which an instrument will be governed",* whereupon the substance of my argument on this subject rest. Since Justice Roberts ruled it unconstitutional if read as a command. Therefore that being said, "if read as a command", consequently it became unconstitutional. Surprise, here comes a second decision by Justice Roberts attempt in order to satisfy the socialist in our republic.

Hence asserting his position from the same Internal Revenue Service code 5000Aa *minimum essential coverage* is therefore constitutional, because it can be reasonably read as a tax, WHAT!

 Please allow me to read section 5000A of the I.R.S. code. *"Requirement (command) to maintain"* that's all no more no less, concluded. *Then the following sections 5000Aa, Ab and Ac could if reasonably read as tax)* nether the word tax or penalty are to be found in sec.5000Aa, although in 5000Ab , 5000Ac of I.R.S. one will find the word penalty on ten occasions but never once tax.
 In the interest of untangling these atrocities, let's act as though we have become delusional following Justice Robert's line of thinking. As we move in his direction we find, the idea of taxes acceptable, *"with regards to the Affordable Care act and this mandate of a tax to punish those who fail to implement the requirement, maintaining minimum essential coverage".* In doing so, I find in our Constitution that excises and taxes must be uniform across our republic. The question seems to me, is Justice Roberts saying that all citizens involved with the Affordable Care Act must pay a uniform excise. The Constitution is very clear on this significant subject, Article one, section eight, first paragraph,

***imposts and excises shall be uniform throughout the United
States*** All taxes except imposts and income tax are excise.

Thus to tax some citizens without taxing all others at the same
rate would be unconstitutional. However, if he's suggesting the tax
is set upon one select group for failing to comply with a *required
minimum essential insurance* coverage, (their words) straight away
that's an entirely new question, such a difficulty to be considered.

If in fact that select group, is in truth punished (taxed) for failure
to comply, thus taxed per John Roberts when failing to comply, has
been restructured into a command, and renovated by fear of
retribution. I am unaware of the ability of the United States
Government to coerce anyone or any group by threat of force to
comply with their wishes. However, John Roberts' notion this act
must be enforced by its exposed stipulation of coercion, thus it
remains unconstitutional on its face, that of exerting a stipulation
of coercion. *As earlier Justice Ginsberg explained to Justice
Roberts, attempting to force any citizen to buy no matter whatever
thing, is unconstitutional. Rather since the congress has the power
to tax, may suggest putting into effect, the word tax in place of the
word penalty.*

Therefore, when a person or groups of persons do in fact comply,
their freedom of choice has been deprived and the Constitution into
an ineffectual document, annulled and void. Which then shall it be
Chief Justice Roberts, one or the other not both, shall the
Constitution rule or you sir. Shall 5000A be read as written a
penalty, or as a tax, if as a tax then failure of complying to a
requirement, merely advocates this fact as a command, thus is
exactly as Justice Ginsburg clearly stated as unconstitutional.
Justice Roberts fails to answer this valid question.

Now it is advocated and written as a penalty, then again we find
within the words written in the transcript of this concept to be
unconstitutional and vocally in the courts own words thus was

obviously their opinion. All the while without qualms, neither interested parties, Congress or the Court repetitively advocated otherwise, on this very questionable issue.

Those, then who controverted the principle that the Constitution is to be considered in court as a paramount law are reduced to the necessity of maintaining that courts must close their eyes on the Constitution, and see only the law, the statute or treaty. "This doctrine would subvert the very foundation of all written constitutions"   Justice Marshal 1803

After this time, 1803 many courts chose to operate using a tactic called Judicial Deference and upon this ideology they became situated to support or defeat the laws by their reading and choosing, moreover by obligatory events, create new laws. Their interpretation of the laws of congress deprived of the influence and authority of our Constitution, gives them crucial choice. Acting upon this idea is unconstitutional.

However, let's go back to where I deviated momentarily, next section 5000Ac called "AMOUNT OF PENALTY" c1, a, b, c2 a-, … on to the next page, four more times I find the word penalty, and how the penalty will be inflicted and how one will be penalized. Their scale for exaction (extortion) for the applicable individual, supposedly we have the m**andate.** Thus Democrats, like Nancy Pelosi House Speaker and Harry Reid leader of the Senate, demanded of their fellow members, their sponsorship. Note: Now an *Applicable Individual* received an additional title**, taxpayer**, under certain conditions in sec.5000Ac, strange how they slink in and changed one's title from "applicable individual", to "taxpayer", how did that happen? The vote was 220-215, all 171 Republicans and 34 Democrats dissented.

Therefore, most of **we the people** possibly believed the Supreme Court generally represented conservative views, instead led by Chief Justice Roberts, with four other Justices,

Ginsburg, Sotomayor, Breyer, and Kagan, all socialist, thus the Affordable Care Act became law. Acting fittingly upon the socialistic ideology and with full intent of supporting the act, "Patient Protection and Affordable Care Act and other things". With deep loathing for our Constitution, not without additional "socialism as well" also coming from President Obama. In true reflection, nothing could possibly be closer to the truth, if it weren't so brutal, it would be a practical joke, a hoax, placed upon our Republic, plus this act is at best a nonentity in value, completed with total deception. If all this sounds as if I'm mangling the ideology of Justice Roberts, it's since I am attacking his line of deception with regards to this particular case and in my opinion a liar, therefore I believe it has not one scintilla of merit. As a result, with consideration to the *Affordable Care Act,* this case is a study in fraud, based upon the I.R.S. Code. These proceedings are called *fraud in law*, contemplation of fraud in law, fraud implied or inferred by law, Fraud by the construction of law. **Perjury** is an example of intrinsic fraud. **1 69 Colo. 70 453, 601**

Thus by means of coercion, one is commanded to take part in a government program, never knowing the results. As the name suggest, "Patient Protection Affordable Care Act **and other things**". Over time I have read most of the Affordable Act and Other Things. We are now beginning to grasp the meaning of Other Things. This is pure and simple fraud commited by those who chose to serve, in essence a mafia style operation, run by the national government's Gestapos, The Supreme Court. I'm sorry, but how does one more appropriately identify these atrocious individuals in power, after properly requesting for, hence swearing to uphold the Constitution.

. As I have previously stated "this is pure and simple fraud commited by those who chose to serve", in principle are crimes commited indisputably, in the operation of our Republic, entirely run by the courts and the congress in union, rather than detached and separate entities.

While on the subject of fraud, again let's go back in history. The era, the great depression less than three out of four workers were earning a few bits of money, others walking the streets, families in soup lines. Sound similar to anything parallel to today, yes you bet. The Congress along with President Roosevelt brought into law Social Security, actuality Workmen's comp., later Unemployment Comp., then Old age insurance, etc., until Social Security. All were established as national insurance programs based on actuarial principles, nationally administered and financed entirely by taxes on employers and employees. It has become an inseparable part of our way of life, Social Security is here to stay. All this was accomplished through a coordinated effort performed by a united Congress, Administration and Courts, at that time called the "New Deal". All this ensued amid a massive depression, nothing but a massive Hoax, controlled by the national government but implemented by the states. Again my opinion, Christian people failed and government moved in and today those programs are failing agendas, bordering on all programs.

Prior to moving forward any further, let's at this late juncture once again define **penalty** and **tax.**

Penalty: The suffering in person or property which is by law, or judicial decision for the commission of a crime, offense or trespass as a punishment. Derived from the word penal...Noah Webster, Inflicting a punishment containing a penalty. Black's law Dictionary.

Tax: A rate or sum of money assessed by government on a person or property of a citizen of state or nation...Noah Webster

A pecuniary burden laid upon individuals or property to support government...Black's law Dictionary

Regretfully I again produce these definitions so late into my argument concerning the Affordable Care Act and the courts impropriety of deliberation from its every conception.

I am confident of my opinion, there are only three probable consequences for one to describe from Justice Robert's decision, with respect to the individual mandate of the Affordable Care Act. One: to establish socialism for the politico. Two: an act of total ignorance and arrogance toward our unalienable rights given by God, Three: a pure fundamental act of dishonesty. Moreover, John Roberts is so erratically confused regarding the issue of law and this statute, this act is confusing to him and beyond belief *"is to protect by whatever method deemed necessary, to keep the law or statue from attack from all possible objections, and furthermore to protect it from an attack by the Constitution"* these are his words which explain his brazen nature.

This man Justice Roberts through his own words, illustrates his plans are as faulty as much of his grasp of the Constitution, and an abundant supply and source of socialist dogma from Barack Obama. I certainly am opposed to this exercise of thought, and I strongly accept the idea that our Constitution *is the* true law of our republic, *the Supreme law being a form which all other laws are guided and obliged to align themselves.* Again the words of Justice Marshal *"I ask if this isn't true then what's the purpose of a constitution, any constitution"?*

Yet again I am obliged to inform Justice Roberts he is mistaken, in fact a Constitution is the established structure or the form a republic state or nation declares, it is which determines if law is true law. Therefore, in our republic all laws are written by the House of Representatives and Senate therefore all laws are essentially compelled to pass the framework of our Constitution, thus this concept gives meaning to our court system, local, state and national. Passing laws willy-nilly would lead to unscrupulous corruption, yet still nothing beyond anything that is confronting us today. In truth, rather not the reality of laws passed currently, as few are established or supported by the Constitution, which is the limit or scope of a statute thereof.

So please Justice Roberts, at a bare minimum, read and study our Founding Fathers, in basic terms learn the meaning and try to appreciate while getting the embodiment of our Constitution. I continue to stress this issue, due to what I see as the importance of its meaning and the very core of our republic's existence.

Chief Justice Marshall in Marbury vs. Madison (1803)

This is of the very essence of judicial duty. If, then, the Courts are to regard the Constitution, and the Constitution is superior to any ordinary act of the Legislature, the Constitution, and not such ordinary act, or case to which they may apply.

Those who controvert the doctrine of our Constitution, as a consequence to be considered in court as the paramount law, therefore reduced the Constitution to the inevitability of maintaining the courts ideology. Consequently the court closes their eyes, no longer seeing the Constitution, rather see only the law [e.g., the statute or treaty].

Which of course is not the opinions or actual positions designed by the framers of our skillfully complete Constitution. However remarkable their work, the description and meaning persists and remain quite clear. Today most of the courts policies would subvert the very foundation of all written Constitutions.

I totally believe the concept of the Constitution's preeminence, whenever, wherever or however the legislators create a law, then the law must meet the purview of the Constitution. Thus the use of such a simplistic idea and is only confusing when it is twisted by those wanting to mutilate and deface its meaning. Please remember the ideology of Thomas Jefferson, *we were endowed by our creator with certain unalienable rights, among them Life, Liberty and the pursuit of happiness, government are instituted among men deriving their just power from the consent of the governed.* Which includes the courts.

Never an idea of having a legislative body to whom we are answerable, or them to themselves singularly, while the courts were only inspired by their own thoughts, thus the law would emerge many times from their meager judgmental ideas, merely as prattling, this without our Constitution to guide them.

Hence our Bible is a guidebook for all persons, which no written law or ideology could dominate. Therefore all other laws regardless from whence they may have taken place, or the issues they may well entail. If this were the progression for congressional law being approved by the courts, then there's no need for a Constitution, but one is there and needed, both the Bible and our Constitution are there for all to read, comprehend for life and attempting to execute.

Here is the mere purpose of our Constitution, while maintaining a check on Congress and the Executive Branch, separate but equal entities at all times. Thus our Constitution is a wall between government and "We the People". Then we find the Bill of Rights, the first Ten Amendments in the Constitution, due to the drafters hindsight, knew their exclusion of certain personal rights would be deficient, never to be permitted by all states, as they were soveriegn.

For decades now the courts at all levels have created law by their decisions, this concept, this objective is to rule our republic from the courtroom. Consequently, in conjunction with a president encompassing all the attributes of a king, nevertheless, a prodigy of the courts, all this and no mention of God Almighty, how far we have fallen since the inception and embodiment of our Constitution.

Accordingly, this is why I have considered it the failure of Christians to press our congress, administration and courts to do the work for which they chose, then elected to serve and execute. I'm well aware and appreciate the fact some Christians and Christian groups are genuinely involved, first in spreading the Gospel of our Lord God and Jesus Christ, then are persistent on influencing the government to think of God in an acquiescent temperament. Hence, following good judgment, essences for intellectual reason and significance of actions by men who, with God's wisdom and help, created our Constitution and this imposing Christian republic.

It's my opinion the courts, in particular the Supreme Court is beyond basic accepted thinking concerning our Constitution, shallow, they deem the Constitution be rewritten as they visit it on a daily basis. How gross my disgust and aversion have I, toward them and just how disconcerting is this outcome and accordingly a need for serious measures taken to combat these unscrupulous persons. I need to be moving on as there are other important ideas and concepts to explore.

The words written in this fourth accusation, were meant to demonstrate how the courts and our Congress are practically one in the same. Plus that the mandate was only a hoax as I am certain it has shown the Justices only lied and misused words to confuse the people after their decision certainly not the court itself. This great statement pertaining to the mandate, put forward by Justice Scalia "if *the government can force one to follow this idea, then they would be able to force you to eat broccoli*". Point being the mandate was nothing but a hoax, a scam on the American people enacted by the Congress and The Supreme Court. I have one more disturbing issue to bring forward for your deliberation. In the much remark on 5000A I find myself incapable of any revealing idea of taxes, only a reference to pl. 111-148 a possible penalty on those refusing the Affordable Care Act. So much about Taxes while the IRS title speaks to penalties and only through pl111-148. This question was never addressed.

Plaintiff's Accusation Fifth Challenge

Our courts willingness to convolute the words in our Constitution

In this section I will attempt to further the argument for an analysis of case law as used by all federal courts, including that of the U.S. Supreme court and Chief Justice Roberts. After reading several with regards to the issue at hand, I became aware of his frustration struggling to gather help in an effort to support his illegal, illogical argument. Exercising this approach rather than a direct interpretation of the Constitution, the court practiced the convoluting of words, slither between other court decisions, not necessarily near or similar to the subject in question. We are obligated to remember Chief Justice is not quite clear, nor how to approach or defend his position.

I would accept this premise, if the solitary objective were to facilitate their application of the Constitution. In my opinion, not to construct an entirely new scheme, able to forfeit those laws and philosophies of our republic's Constitution. As I am firmly convinced our Constitution unquestionably means today, as the day it was written. It was not in the heart of those wise and brave men, inspired by God to imagine otherwise. Only foolish men attempt to controvert and change meanings to fit their entangled judgments. As always, these are case laws used by Justice Roberts striving for support of his lies, penalty vs. tax being analogous, synonymous words, rather remaining quite untrue.

For myself, the meaning is quite clear in **Gibbons vs. Ogden** (1822) 22 U.S.1 a case Justice Roberts strolls out, but seems unable to clearly figure out or comprehend its meaning.

Gibbons vs. Ogden... More of Justice Robert's misconception and misuse of case law.

"If, as always has been understood, the sovereignty of Congress, though limited to specified objects, is plenary as to those objects, the power over commerce with foreign nations and among the several states is vested in Congress as absolutely as it would be in a single government, having in its Constitution the same restrictions on the exercise of the power as are found in the Constitution of the United States."
I discovered not a hint of suggestion to change words or meaning of the written Constitution, or for integrating any other significance or connotations as to the statements rendered earlier by Justice Marshall.

In addition case law was not a practice in the early eighteen hundreds, the Constitution being the base line used in the determination of their decisions, why the courts strayed is open to question. Nevertheless, Justice Roberts again pilfers, boosting his personal untruthful advocacy.

U.S. vs. Halper 490 U.S. 435...More Justice Robert's case law, *relying primarily on United States v. Halper, 490 U. S. 435 (1989), the Bankruptcy Court decided that the assessment constituted a form of double jeopardy. The court rejected the_State's argument* ***that the tax was not a penalty*** *because it was designed to recover law_enforcement costs; as the court noted, the DOR "failed to introduce one scintilla of evidence as to cost of the above government programs or costs of law enforcement incurred to combat illegal drugs.*

This case was about taxes and double jeopardy, nowhere within the disposition of the case were there considerations for the meaning of, words or alterations of the same.

The courts determination as it was a penalty thus not a tax.

Kurth Ranch 511 U.S.   Again Justice Robert's case law.

*A legislature's description of gain a statute as civil does not foreclose the possibility that it has a punitive character, and that a defendant convicted and punished for an offense may not have a non- remedial civil penalty imposed against him for the same offense in a separate proceeding, the Court did not consider whether a tax may similarly be characterized as punitive. However, the Court's recognition that the extension of **a so called tax penalizing feature can cause it to lose its character as such and become a mere penalty.***

This case is solely on the subject of taxes, taxes levied by the state of Montana. Again no argument or discussion of altering the meaning of words because Justice Roberts seems to believe penalty is simply the same as tax, were not an issue in this case.

I have read several cases in this regard, some used by Justice Roberts but he was unable to find where the word penalty and tax are synonymous, in fact it never appeared in the same paragraph. Subsequently, whichever these Justices supposed, they are either ignorant of the use of these words or just exploited their meaning.

Never citing or applying the Constitution other than the Congress use of the taxing clause. On the other hand the use of an application of the law itself was never argued or objections confronted by this panel of Supreme Court Justices as in the argument over Affordable Care Act. This case, **Kurth Ranch 511 U.S.** existed concerning growing marijuana in the state of Montana. Ultimately the owner of the ranch was taxed per pound of the illegal plant. There never was an issue of word changing or synonymous meaning. Justice Roberts's case is without merit and on its very face must be recognized as such. This case totally inerrant to Justice John Roberts use as an issue, unquestionably outside of the " **Kurth Ranch 511 U.S.**" case. The Kurth Ranch was taxed per pound of marijuana grown as that was Montana's means to control the growing of marijuana.

In Parsons vs. Bedford- 28 U.S. 448. Case of 1830   Another Justice Roberts attempt at case law used in his misguided ideology.

"If indeed, the construction contended for at the bar were to be given to the act of Congress, we entertain the most serious doubts whether it would not be unconstitutional. No court ought, unless the terms of an act rendered it unavoidable, to give a construction to it which should involve a violation, however unintentional of the Constitution. The terms of the present act may well be satisfied by limiting its operation to modes of practice and proceeding in the court below without changing the effect or conclusiveness of the verdict of the jury upon the facts litigated at the trial".

This is simply a portion of this case, moreover from reading further gave no reason or intent to suppose otherwise. I could find nothing to support Justice Roberts own opinions, while taking into account the Affordable Care Act. However it began without concept of, or in anyway was a communal thought in his effort in presenting case law.

HOOPER v. PEOPLE STATE OF CALIFORNIA, 155 U.S. 648 1895 No. 7 January 7, 1895 Section 623 of the Political Code of the state of California provides as follows: For each insurance company, association, firm or individual for whose account it is proposed to collect premiums of insurance in this state. The condition of such bond to be applied as follows: First, *"That the person or firm, agent or officer named therein, acting on*

*behalf of the company, association, firm or individual, named
therein, will pay to the treasurer of the county, or city and county
in which the principal office of the agency is located, such sum per
quarter, quarterly in advance, for a license to transact an
insurance business or such other license".* **[155 U.S. 648, 649]**
As may be imposed by law as long as the agency remains in the
hands of the person or firm, agent or officer named as principal in
the bond.

*Second. That the person or firm, officer or agent will pay to the
state all stamp or other duties on the gross amounts insured
inclusive of renewals on existing policies.*
*Third. That the person, firm, agent or corporation named therein
will conform to all provisions of the revenue or other laws made to
govern them.'*

While reading the above, one readily discovers this case refers to
insurance and how it need be applied in the state of California, the
agents and or firm representing a company association, etc. etc.

None of the above case has any resemblance to the case of which
we are concerned, the above case never presents any lawyers or
Justices as referring in any way to taxes, although a few instances
are made regarding penalties, only in relationship to the penal
code, with the possibility of being guilty of a misdemeanor.

This case was eighteen plus pages long and has no influence what
so ever regarding the Affordable Care Act, nor does it as Justice
Roberts suggest, the government asked to interpret the case
(Hooper vs. state **of California**) as a mandate to tax, as it would
otherwise violate the Constitution. Granting the Act the full
measure of deference owed to federal statues, it can be so read, for
the reasons set forth below. Please remember this California case
was tried in California.

Does he assume we are all fools, I have with others read this case **Hooper vs. California** three times, nowhere does the government request we frame this case as to read it as a mandate imposing a tax, the word "tax" would never even fit this case which as I stated and one can read for themselves, it is about insurance, agents, firms, companies which involves insurance for large ships, etc., etc. with regards to California state law.

I am irritated, more to the point infuriated when he reaches so far, leading one to momentarily question their own reliability to grasp the proceedings.

Again I am of the opinion Justice Roberts continues to reach in the extreme in order to support his ridiculous ideology, attempting to avoid the truth, using case law, rather than first an application of our Constitution. Reading Justice Roberts decision directly from the transcripts, one detects a feeling of desperation coming from his quoting case law to the extreme, grasping at straws, reminiscent of Don Quixote chasing his windmills, at any rate Justice Roberts is in no way "the man of La Mancha". The case directly above has no value for the situation regarding the Affordable Care Act, there is no merit on its face fitting to support Justice John Roberts's contentions. Of course his ideology is in opposition to many of his other decisions, lacking surprise? **United States vs. Reorganized & Fabricators 95-325**

The District Court and the Tenth Circuit affirmed. Held:1. The "tax" under § 4971 (a) was not entitled to second eight, Article One priority as an "excise tax" under § 507(a)(7)(E), but instead is, for bankruptcy purposes, a penalty to be dealt with as an ordinary, unsecured claim. Pp. 218-226. Congress included no such reference in [§507(a)(7)(E)], even though the bankruptcy code. Code provides no definition of "excise", "tax," or "excise tax." This absence of any explicit connection between [§§ 501 507(a)(7)(E) and 4971] is all the more revealing in light of this

Court's history of interpretive practice in determining whether a "tax" so called in the statute creating it is also a "tax" for its purpose.

The Court's cases in this area looks to whether the purpose of an exaction in support of the government or punishment for an unlawful act. If the concept of a penalty means anything, it means punishment for an unlawful act or omission. That is what this exaction is **[4971]**. The exaction is imposed for violating a separate federal statute requiring the funding of pension plans, and thus obviously has no penal character. **[Pp. 224-225].** The complaint, judgment was entered for the company against the collector IRS for the full amount, with interest. The writ of error is prosecuted by the collector direct from the District Court under section 238 of the Judicial Code (**Comp. St. 1215**).... and later approved a reorganization plan for CF&I giving lowest priority and (no money) to claims regarding non-compensatory penalties.

There are twenty pages presented for the decision of this case, again I could not find within the resolution of the court, anywhere stated they could justify the use of twisting words by the court to correspond with the intent of the law, presented by Congress. The facts of this case were argued on the merits of excise taxes and state rights, the Ninth and Tenth amendments primarily. This case decided three points. **One**, the IRS was not within the essence of its authority, **two**, the congress had improperly exercised its agenda in this case, **three**, the case should have been under the jurisdiction of state laws in accordance with the Constitution at the Tenth amendment, the sovereignty of the state and its people.

U.S. Supreme BAILEY v. DREXEL FURNITURE CO., 259 U.S. 20 (1922)

Argued March 8, 1922. Decided May 15, 1922. [259 U.S. 20, 21] Mr. Solicitor General Beck, of Washington D. C., for plaintiff in error. [259 U.S. 20, 28] Mr. Wm. P. Bynum, of

Greensboro, N. C., for defendant in error. [259 U.S. 20, 34] Chief Justice TAFT delivered the opinion of the Court.

This case presents the question of the constitutional validity of the Child Labor Tax Law. The plaintiff below, the Drexel Furniture Company, is engaged in the manufacture of furniture in the Western district of North Carolina. On September 20, 1921, it received a notice from Bailey, United States collector of internal revenue for the district and that it had been assessed [**$6,312.79**] for having during the taxable year 1919 employed and permitted to work in its factory a boy under 14 years of age, thus incurring the tax of 10 per cent on its net profits for that year. The company paid the tax under protest, and, after rejection of its claim for a refund, brought this suit. On demurrer to an amended complaint, judgment was entered for the company against the collector for the full amount, with interest. The writ of error is prosecuted by the collector direct from the District Court under **section 238 of the Judicial Code (Comp. St. 1215**

I concluded from this case the IRS attempted in error to collect a tax, instead of the government charging Drexel Furniture in the question of validity with regards to their action with the "child labor tax law". I identified no questions concerning an issue of taxes other than the IRS mistakenly collecting a tax illegally and a penalty was never in question. Thus as for our purpose, the issue with regards to this case is lacking support or merit.

As in all the cases I brought to your attention, you can find them in full in most law history books the terms in Black's law Dictionary. Noah's Dictionary of American English Language for the meaning of words used. I was fortunate enough to have the orginal transcripts and copies of Justice Roberts' case laws, which simplified the task somewhat, thus gave me the opportunity and great break to serve you with the proper information.

Plaintiff's Accusation Sixth Challenge

Additionally and must be seen as foremost, the National Government's power is limited by our Constitution plus the Bill of Rights, especially concerning the Ninth and Tenth Amendments. Regarding those stating the sovereignty of all states and its people are supreme. In fact the National government must adhere to all of the amendments in our Bill of Rights. Where in the Constitution has the National Government been given the power to control the choice of the people, or it's state and people forced into purchasing **anything**, let alone insurance to cover one's own health.

I have faith in the American people to deem what is best for themselves and their families, not some outrageous political hacks in Washington D.C. I challenge any politician to confront and deny this statement, especially, Nancy Pelosi, Harry Reid and President Obama, who knows now we have only fifty states not fifty seven. Justice Roberts, what you are looking for **just does not exist.** Regardless, if I or any person or persons had the opportunity to challenge these cases or others like them, they would only lie, more smoke and mirrors or act as if we the people are not capable of comprehending the complete picture simultaneously. Let me read you from *The Fifth Amendment, section four, "nor be deprived of Life Liberty or property, without due process of law"*.

The affordable Care Act deprives us these God given rights. Plus the entire Seventh Amendment. Mr. Noah Webster *"In United States the unwritten law, the law that receives its binding force from time long-established usage and universal reception,*

all come from God, in distinction from the written law or statute."
This coming from man.

One could go on endlessly with this ill-advised activity, but to what end. The point of case law, actually accomplished by staffers, is meant to help with their opinion regarding the subject's substance. The fact we have a Constitution is secondary at best, in spite of this We the People move on aimlessly, accepting our loss of freedoms as if there is no recourse. While scores of persons unaware or are unacquainted concerning the facts, nor knowledge of these facts are realized, save for a small number. In our Constitution and its great predecessor the Declaration of Independence, without which there would be no Constitution, in my opinion accomplished by an undersized number of honest and wise men, supported by God, giving us a Constitution unlike any other. There are but few recognizing all our freedoms come from God, governments simply embezzles and acquires by default our liberty, doing so by an awe-inspiring method. Words possessed with absolute significance during the writing of the U.S. Constitution. I am of the conviction it **was** these rights' where Justice Roberts avoids the truth, or persist in acting merely dismissive of the truth, or was so perplexed and confused as where to present his ideology, his single presentation.

Ben Franklin, when asked with respect to what the convention was about " *a Constitution if you will keep it"* I ask, how could we have gotten so far from God and country.

I've gotten off the point, back to Justice Roberts and the other Justices, Ginsburg, Breyer, Sotomayor and Kagan, whom never having adjudicated a case, till being appointed to the Supreme Court in 2009 as they are presently our concern. Justice Roberts stated that the shared responsibility as payments are not a penalty but a tax. Then he, Justice Roberts argued in the Anti-Injunction Act with regards to the Affordable Care Act it was a penalty not a tax, as this was Constitutional.

Visit Section 5000A (b). To the extent Justice Roberts manipulates the meaning of this section and that according to this section creates a mandate, thus establishing a condition while not owning health insurance will trigger a tax, the required payment headed for the IRS. Under that theory, the mandate is not a legal command to buy insurance, rather, it makes going without insurance just another thing the government taxes, like buying gasoline, taxed, or purchasing tobacco, taxed which you purchase by choice and pay the tax, by choice. And if the mandate is in effect just like a tax on certain taxpayers who do not purchase health insurance, those who chose not to buy it are without insurance, like those who made the other choices. The question is not whether that is the most natural interpretation of the mandate, as it is, but only whether it is a "deceitfully possible" one.

The question is not a matter of mandate (command) as the government cannot command you to do anything whatever, unless in the service of the military when in actual service in time of war or public danger. Again I submit, they suggest their power in law and reading of the Constitution and to its conclusion is *Judicial Deference.* Nowhere in the Constitution is there such a suggestion or thought, this is merely a fabrication, figment of their imagination and desire for power.

Otherwise, as to the point Justice Scalia said "if so they could force you to eat broccoli" guessing he is not a broccoli fan, I love that assertion.

I find we the people, are so anemic and pathetic to locate persons capable of serving in our government who are devoid of corruption and truly willing to serve. Are they not to be found?

Crowell v Benson, 285 U.S. 2, 62 (1932); Returning to the words of one Chief Justice John Roberts, "if read reasonably it could fairly possible read tax". Of course this is not the most reasonable, his own words, and furthermore it is only "unfairly possible". Nowhere in the case, **Crowell v Benson** does it suggest, in any way that one can read the meaning of any word essential to the case into whatever one wishes to twist its meaning. Furthermore, in **Crowell v Benson** does it suggest that any essential word or words, where one argues what is natural and another possible exist as one together. However, the words "most natural", and whether it is "fairly possible" are not the same as the actual word. As for penalty, which is the word written in 5000 A (b) and tax being imaginative. The words penalty and tax have entirely different meanings, one, penalty is defined for doing something wrong while taxes are established through Article One sec. 8 and its enumerated topics, sadly many other schemes to deprive the people of their hard work, only to create programs undesirable to the majority of the folks.

Then Justice Roberts stated the issue in the Affordable Care Act is the same as the cigarettes tax which is used as revenue as well as a preventive issue. Now Justice Roberts declares the government profits from these taxes but also to thwart smoking to some degree. The habit of smoking remains a matter of choice, even while an impediment for smoking may occur to a lesser degree. The desire of smoking is a matter of choice, of which one knowingly choses to pay the taxes and smoke, as I have enumerated previously. Then is that idea suggested in 5000A, 5000Aa, 5000Ab and 5000Ac, or is it anywhere? There are no such national laws preventing one from smoking, thus there is no penalty attached for doing what one wishes, only the attached tax which the person choses to pay by their choice for smoking.

Again he addresses taxes, cunningly in a direct manner, as he has chosen to elect gasoline as a tax paid without choice if one wishes to purchase fuel. At the pump one makes a conscious choice, without a law to ponder, merely shall I bring into being a purchase? Once I choose to purchase fuel I agree to pay the tax, no influence by government, no penalty, just the need for fuel, or buy a bicycle.

I am a simple man asking simple questions, typically to seek the truth through our God given Rights, not though volumes of useless words contained in buildings, contrived by incompetent, bungling party persons. Likewise, Justice Roberts attempts an analogy of cigarettes and gasoline with the Affordable Care Act, where I make a distinction, a competent comparison, as Justice John Roberts' remarks were simply unwise, only the lack of choice being the issue at hand, here illuminated.

I believe the Affordable Care Act to be as Senator DeMint states *"violates beyond the rule of law"*. We find on page 1001 of the act *"reduce the per capita rate of growth"* raise revenues on Medicare beneficiary premiums under section **1818, 1818a, or 1839** sounding as if their idea of not rationing is a lie, while it seems to me as they simply never had any intention to pay, long or short term.

So much for the sufficiency and consideration for the people of the union of the United States, that of Obama Care. We are still not told or are to understand what "and other things" mean, if or when they take place. I suggest their meaning, Blank. Blank and Blank, merely open to any and all future ideas.

Chapter Seven

Must the Declaration of Independence Still be of Importance?

Our Declaration of Independence was an intentional list of grievances, against a degenerate monarch, King George III, and between the colonists who disagreed with his rule are long dead. The ideology promoted by Samuel Adams and written primarily by Thomas Jefferson also spoken by Patrick Henry for the cause which led to this declaration, it read in part, *"If ye love wealth better than liberty, the tranquility of servitude than the animating contest of freedom, go from us in peace. We ask not your counsels or arms. Crouch down and lick the hands which feed you. May your chains sit lightly upon you, and may posterity forget that ye were our countrymen".*

Still voluminous the persons which exist today, including numerous politicians, proclaiming the Constitution and our Republic as a democracy, how far from reality. Their ignorance of our Republic's history is part of the schools failed system, to our children and beyond.

Still many continue living in a fog today, countless of those people who continue to argue that the Declaration is obsolete. In fact, this is exactly what those who called themselves "progressives", better socialist, were saying more than a century ago. President Woodrow Wilson, one of the most infamous early progressives, argued during the 1912 presidential campaign that all that Progressives asked, their desire was for the *"permission to interpret the Constitution according to the Darwinian principle,"* meaning that it should promote an ever expanding set of powers for an ever-expanding government and atheistic in principle.

The problem he declared, was that pesky Declaration of Independence. An array of citizens from our republic have never gotten beyond *Life, Liberty and the Pursuit of Happiness* found within the Declaration of Independence. Yet this is what pleases their desire. The certainty of a fixed point in time, our Declaration of Independence was meant to be static, fixed and constant. As the statements in this document remains the same today, especially with the facts, viewing the considerations of our current plight. Somewhat liken to the Bible, its facts never grow old nor its principles diminish with time. The Ten Commandments are still the greatest guide for all to follow, attempt and struggle with living.

But in fact the Declaration is more than a litany of complaints. Its greater meaning is a statement of the conditions of legitimate political authority and the proper ends of government. It proclaimed that political rule would, from then on, reside in the sovereignty of the people. *"If the American Revolution had produced nothing but the Declaration of Independence,"* wrote the great historian Samuel Eliot Morrison, *"it would have been worthwhile."*

The ringing phrases of the document's famous second paragraph are a powerful synthesis of American constitutional and republican form of government theories. All men *have a right to life, liberty* however as they are by The Declaration, it also insists we have the right to *"the pursuit of happiness."* A higher component of that pursuit, of course, is being able to worship as we please. This right is our fundamental religious liberty. Yet that right seems to be under attack today by our government alongside many others. When will the American people be willing to defend that right, our God given rights and repair our republic to its authentic and accurate beginnings, a people believing with an objective of "*a people who are called by my name, will humble themselves and pray and seek my face and turn from their wicked ways, then will I hear from heaven and will forgive their sin and will heal their land*" 2nd Chronicles (7:14)

I firmly believe that George Washington's faith in God, made him the absolute and utterly complete military General, leading a small band of non-professional soldiers to thwart the most powerful military force at that time. Furthermore, his presidency was without a doubt one of the finest we as a people have ever possessed and honored, also he was the finest political leader ever.

The Supreme Court's decision to uphold the Affordable Care Act reflects a tragic misreading of the Constitution and the law, such which could cost us not just economic troubles, but also in terms of liberty. On the bright side, the Court recognized that there are limits to what Congress may do under the Commerce Clause. But this was the silver-lining of a very dark cloud. The Court then fundamentally misreads the Affordable Care act, contorting facts to find another authority, as the power to tax was designed for the Congress's ability to impersonate the laws. The distress of this decision will be felt far beyond The Affordable Care Act, as the courts deception was beyond description and Justice John Roberts multiple of absolutely incredible lies, will plague him.

Thanks for the Heritage Foundation and for their marching to the same beat as mine, makes one feel like they and I are not the only ones in defense of our Republic, despite the fact that defense of it **should not** ever have become necessary.

The Constitution, and the largest part of all, reinforcing and bringing God Almighty back into our governmental system and society.

On a political note, I absolutely believe we need a president rather like George Washington, rather essentially we are in need of a man whose source and convictions come from God, with God given exceptional qualities. Strong hearted men like Washington, Jefferson, Franklin, Adams, Monroe and Patrick Henry, on and on. We need not a new country, but an old country, the republic from which we originated. One, great men fought for and two, a God given gift to we the people, a great republic, where is that republic today? Our country was Christian based and had only one God, it was pluralistic only in the sense of theological approach.

When will the adult Americans awaken and enlighten our young children of a clear understanding and responsibility to our Constitution. I am unquestionably correct it should be explained and taught very early in the school years and reimbursed through the higher institutions of learning. Today it's we who are a shamelessly, blatantly and ignorant generation, both constitutionally and politically, we have little if any knowledge of our Republic, while we hear the politicians speak of our democracy. **We are not a Democracy but a Republic** as I have explained before. We the people are the Government, not a Democratic system which is merely mob rule.

Theology existence, occurs in four well-defined distinctions: one… *Divinity* the science of God and divine things. Two… *morality*, divine laws and moral duties. Three… being, *speculative* teaching us the objects of faith. Four… *scholastics* that which teaches by reasoning of the principles of faith. There were several approaches in different organizations, while all were Christians, believing in God and His Son Jesus Christ, His death and resurrection to pardon our sins.

I feel it necessary, in a well-defined matter to establish the correct words rather than those so often spoken, the incorrect idea of "well those people in Washington" as if there is some magical group of persons to lay blame upon. Well I'm here to tell all, there is only you and I to blame when reason seem out of our control, I still suggest just you and I are here to fix or change those factors. We chose the people we send to meet in Washington to represent our interest and our needs, if indeed our state is incapable. If they are unsuccessful and changing people does not succeed, there is yet another answer at Article five, read it, it's a Constitutional Convention held by the state Legislators or by a convention itself amending, thus creating a new Constitution. May I say, stop whining and complaining and do something.

This summing-up of reason, is specifically designated for those who may call themselves Christians, as they should be out front leading the way for the repair of our broken government. At this time ISIS above all needs our intense and relentless force, there is a need to change our combative posture, becoming extremely more aggressive in the middle-east, which includes Iran and Syria. It is irrational for us teaming up with Iran for any reason. What I believe one must first pray, then kill them! As their ruthless brutal goal is to kill us and anyone who doesn't agree with their cold-blooded objectives, using some merciless religion as their perverse reasoning, is cold hearted individual and truly a fool.

I have also made clear, the fact the Quran is a fake, noting that roughly 35 verses that command Muslims to murder Jews and Christians who get in the way of Islam's jihad. The evidence in the Mid- East seems to support Dr. Jeffress position, as ISIS continues to slaughter Christians. This persists with little opposition in words or action from the President of the United States, he is incapable or unwilling to call out the perpetrators, still failing to call them for what they are, extreme Islamic terrorist and perhaps not only the so called extreme Islam.

Now we are giving Iran 150 BILLION dollars as a reward for signing an agreement while we knelt before them giving away the farm, "so to speak", as of yet they have not signed., as if it would matter. Why should we consider negotiations, we are in a strong position to demand, furthermore, Iran built their strength by lying and continue to create terrorism through the Middle-East and Northern Africa. Meanwhile the Ayatollah Khamenei carries on calling for death to the Jews and the great Satan United States and we should give them 150 Billion dollars. Even Neville Chamberlain didn't give Hitler a signing bonus, Obama breaks new ground daily. This man Obama, is either the chief architect of buffoonery we ever had visited upon us, or a fool allocating innumerable funds to ever failing ideas, as if government was in business. Every public endeavor has been a boondoggle, his ability to implant, or guide in facilitating foreign affairs has been one disaster after another disaster. The only other answer, he is intent on destroying this nation as a Christian republic. Let's remember I have been critical of his early education was through Muslim teaching. One can question easily see his lack of love for America and why he persists to defend the Islamic ideology, regardless of the mealy-mouth lying words coming out from between his lips.

Now he, Obama has entered into a compact with Iran over their nuclear build up. An episode not approved by congress nor supported by the American people, nevertheless he has moved ahead with the support of the U.N. and the European nations. The aftermath of this accord, without any doubt is horrendous to the free world, thus this agreement must be terminated.

Since details don't categorically dispense substance, the contract unquestionably does.

It is at the heart of an argument over the character of U.S. leadership in the Middle East. Therefore it becomes significant and central due to the obvious implications and may come to be adrift in the struggle over centrifuges and enrichment percentages. We find President Obama and his Iranian deal, the centerpiece of his poorly recommended instruction, concerning the nuclear non-proliferation struggles, his effort to pull the United States from its earlier commitment in the destructive struggles of the region. He Obama, seeking to re-establish the United States as a balance in the arena of the middle east, rather than as an open participant in its endless civil wars. United States has few true friends, with plenty of true enemies which many are able and willing to join. I realize that the U.S. supports Iranian goals in Iraq, all the while supporting Iranian opponents in Yemen". It's so apparent while lack of a moral compass, their loosely used ideals by U.S. and its allies, only entangling them further in their disputes with Iran. This conundrum has befallen upon our nation through deprived, inferior leadership by President Obama, and a more often than not, a deficient congress and you plus myself, allowed this situation to exist.

I must move on to the third part of my trilogy, trying to expose the many problems facing our republic and the answer.

The sovereignty and safety of our republic and its citizen are at risk, whither they grasp it or not, moreover the lack of God Almighty in our society allows socialism to enter the vacuum left by the absence of God and His leadership plus His very presence. This nation as with all nations, God Almighty must reside in that nation, both its people and government (the people) in order to maintain a sense of moral integrity. I believe the problem within our society stems from self-indolence in so many ways. Weak Christians revealed by the many near empty churches, and a good number of pastors displaying an anemic account of Jesus Christ and teaching them His redeeming love. Furthermore, our present government's attack on Christianity comes from all directions as well, in which again stems from socialism. Pray Almighty God, it would please Him to pardon all our manifold sins and transgressions and finally establish the peace and freedom of America, set upon a solid and lasting foundation."

Once more for definite clarity on the issue of penalty verses Tax.

U.S. SUPREME COURT at 259
U.S. 20 Bailey vs. Drexel
Furniture Co.
Decided May15, 1922... Syllabus

> *An act of Congress which clearly on its face, is designed to penalize, and hereby to discourage or suppress, conduct the regulation of which is reserved by the Constitution exclusively to the states, cannot be sustained under the federal taxing power by calling the **penalty** a **tax**.* As I have appropriately explained.

Chapter Eight

Criminal charges against Barrack Obama which are essential and appropriate.

Upon an honest and factual examination, a segment of government designed for a three shared responsibility, rather they have turned into utter corruption, courts were designed to safeguard our Constitution. My accusations regarding the Affordable Care Act, exposing Chief Justice John Roberts as an example of travesty and perversion at the highest levels. Our past president therefore while laying barefaced, exposing where government has been unmasked, both correctly and objectively. Thus resulting in giving you the reader, a clear explanation of how this particular act came to fruition. Subsequently, through corruption and proven to be propagated by lies and deception from the mouth of Chief Justice John Roberts and Justices Ginsburg, Breyer, Sotomayor and Kagan along with countless other political individuals, defaming our Republic.

Therefore, Justice Roberts has not only exposed himself as a liar, rather in addition a few facts and enough to adjudicate those facts which have been written. Some by brilliance, others honesty and challenging work. Mine established through *fait Justitia* against Chief Justice John Roberts. He, writing the assenting decision on cases, docs. *11-398, 11-393, 1-400* all involving all parts of the Patient Protection and Affordable Car Act and Other Things. In particular with the utmost significance, **"the individual mandate"**. Anyone reading my presentation today and studying our history, therefore it subsists with indisputable evidence, as one of many noteworthy finds, as just how numerous cases the Supreme Court has convoluted through manipulation and in other instances through outright lies. Many of these individuals in black robes have held sovereignty for themselves. Therefore being of a contrary mind, while feigning allegiance to our Constitution and many through their actions have only diminished our Constitution and thus in particular failed the American people once again.

I carefully and in an exhausting manner, spent an abundance of time endeavoring to share specific objectives for an America of past ideals, given to us by God. Therefore expecting those beliefs would direct our nation's path toward a careful selection onto a healthier thus once again a Christian Republic. This selection which will rekindle that salient desire, a hunger for our lost republic, not terminated rather merely lost. This ideology will again bring the yearnings for freedom and liberty back to all, as it remains alive. Conversely, as a demonstration that we have unalienable rights, granted by God our ultimate leader, not government nor society, significantly our entire destiny, as a matter of fact is His will. Thus being the impetus for us to seize and secure personal freedoms, thus savoring them once more, these are ours to recapture.

While our Constitution has fallen into the hands of those who wish to trash it, thus to the point of being invalid, regardless of what politicians from either side claim and not by accident, especially those who are wishing to convert our Republic's intended objective.

Past President Obama's attempt to sell you on the idea that we are a democracy, nevertheless our Constitution exist and we are a Republic, granted to us by the God of His universe.

What's more God bestowed upon us unalienable rights, AMONG them Life, Liberty and the pursuit of happiness. These words are solidified and guaranteed, granting us total freedom, freedom from government as they are meant to be our servant, since it's a government of the people, by the people, for the people. We have been designed by God to be the masters of our future according to His guide lines, government being our servant, is meant to follow the wishes and demands from "We the People".

Rather today as I have stated previously, one must connect this truth to ourselves, government is a poor and unfaithful servant, unfortunately a true masquerade for the national government. As a result the situation appears the same, while the national government's determined to extinguish our Constitution and enslave the people with decrees, regulations and ultimately more important, trashing the word of God attempting to destroy Christianity, it being our Republic's foundation. The protests, rioting, and insane response to the police in Ferguson has simply escalated overnight, but Fox & Friends invited **Jonathan Gentry**, a minister whose **rant** went viral (a poor word used to express his implicit message) thus criticizing the black community for not obeying the police. His words are straight to the point, something which President Barack Obama should have furnished, several days prior.

Gentry wrote lately on his Facebook page: A Man said to him *"You're dragging us blacks down!" I said sir, "You can't possibly go any lower than where you already are. You come to my Facebook page, I'm Stepping Your Game Up!! The reason you hate me is because I don't cater to your ignorance and degenerate mindset. Enough is simply Enough, It's your own actions & behavior that's keeping you bound, stuck, not getting ahead. Everything you stood for went down the drain last night by burning down your own community".*

"Your iniquities have turned these blessings away, and your sins have kept good from you." (Jeremiah 5:25) "I'm going to tell you what you need to hear as opposed to what you want to hear. All

we know how to do is blame the police and white folks for our actions. All we know how to do is protest by marching, riot and loot. I'm sick of it! I'm sick of it!". Simply put these words are true for all Americans, the method of our actions may be expressed by different means, but before God there is no difference and they persist in bringing the same feeble and pathetic arguments, I mean both black and white persons.

Please, if nothing else remember Jesus Christ is our redeemer, individually and as a nation, there is none other. When one wishes to protest, bring your protest before God first. It would appear there are many who would seek to twist the truth, leading us down a slippery path, our Republic in chaos thus into obliteration. While many bandits waiting to suck the life out of those persons looking for the passage to freedom. The answers are all written in the Bible and our Constitution. What demands do we find for this subject to materialize? This compels all of us, first to follow the Bible's demands to follow Christ example and our leaders to follow our lead, as the people are the true leaders.

Moving ahead, President Obama being the true architect of deliberate false statements, without question a perpetrator of lies and a man devoid of morals. Furthermore, in his earlier years was thoroughly engaged as a student and disciple of Saul Alinsky (a gangster and a member of the old Al Capone mob), Hillary Clinton as well, perhaps even more so, writing her college thesis and dissertation on his life and ideas, whom she esteemed while praising him for his revolutionary line of reasoning and contentions.

An example of words from one Saul Alinsky *"The rules make the difference between being a realist radical and being a rhetorical one, advancing ones radical goals by camouflaging them, change your style to appear to be working within the system".* Simply looking around one will easily see this theory in play today, mainly by the President, as he has often spoken words knowing they were lies, in so many cases attempting to manipulate their meaning. The terrorist ISIS employ the same ideology as Saul Alinsky. Place this on your calendar, I believe him, Obama, to be a plausible, blooming prospect for becoming the precursor to the anti-Christ.

We need to take control of the national government's abuse of the Constitution, knowing those who cherry-pick it, while choosing to exploit the laws they themselves passed. Furthermore, we must not allow government to manipulate our faiths, ideas and activities, therefore taking away our soveriegnty by subjugation, thus stealing our true source of strength through faith in God, the same God which gave wisdom and power to the founders of this once great Republic, yearning again for His will to become our strength.

Consequently, I have chosen to apply the same implication of prosecution by *Fiat Justitia*, as previously were applied in opposition to Justice John Roberts's deceptive opinions.

Even though there exist a generous supply of infractions by our past President acting outside the law and over reaching his authority, plus there is an abundant amount of exploitations for him to defend presently. Nevertheless, an example of his crimes, violations and infractions of laws, as he has commited them still exist to be examined.

These proceedings are from a substantial list of absolute lawlessness, a **modus injuria.** The only priorities found are the overabundance of illegal issues he indulged himself, the selection of egregious measures we have chosen, yet are from such an abundant list, so much so that it becomes problematic. We have decided upon those from not only laws he has broken, but laws which he failed to apply and enforce. This covers many duties and debt to the Constitution. For that reason the people of our Republic need to realize how voluminous his crimes.

Moreover, believing the significance of injury to our citizens becomes first and foremost, the utmost of substantive questions, though this may depend upon a person's individual prospective, as to what, where or who and the adverse damage Obama has willfully inflicted, while he has hustled up many criminal activities. The ones I have chosen are but a few of those which possibly will be exposed. I hope these will paint a picture of an immoral heart within this man, one Barack Obama, who is not a Negro, rather a Mulatto, merely a man playing a Negro a man with a white mother. Pursuing the Negro votes and espousing their needs as a Black, but doing nothing, he simply is a ***perfidious one***, Latin for betrayal of trust.

Hence in my judgment, I see Mr. Obama as a psychopathic, motivated person, and so characterized by his delusional fantasies, these generally stem from some belief system, where he judges by fiat, thus blaming America for the wrongs in the world, for reason of its power and influence in world affairs. His feeling of omnipotence, further showing his obsession with himself and his grandiose ideas, therefore being a reckless person, a true megalomaniac.

I have read the above statement several times to revisit the words, considering all the issues involved. As for myself, each fits Obama's character and personality, are an absolute projection of this very flawed person. Nevertheless, I am myself a sinful person, finding myself carrying out sinful gambits and deeds, then again I am a Christian and God through His mercy will forgive, rather I pray for His forgiveness and attempt with His help to improve, therefore being remorseful.

I see no repentance in any of his actions, on the contrary Obama as President is obligated, as a result of his own actions, choses to be meritoriously held to the highest of standards, these rules and concepts are broken, existing so without exception.

I will commence with my charges against Mr. Obama in *Fait Justitia,* exposing his lawless behavior, hence the essential need for so many prerequisites for having been removed from office. Therefore, after my charges, I have no expectation for impeachment, as he is gone, the Supreme Court must bring charges of treason, as the man is a traitor to our Republic. Regardless, I was never in anticipation of any reality for impeachment proceedings. As our congress is without the drive, never having the fortitude to exercise same, thus he is walking the streets as a free man.

Moving forward Mr. Obama is a free American citizen and remains yet answerable to the charges I bring forth against him. Mr. Obama is without the problem of impeachment, however he is not free from the law and the charges stand. Each charge brought should be sustained and continued in a criminal court. He like any other common criminal must answer for his behavior and unlawful activities. Therefore I will move forward.

First accusation

This concerns Mr. Obama's failure to maintain his oath of office.

When one is charged with perjury the individual must have had lied while under oath, thus the grounds for many of past President Obama's lies, to become perjury, as he was under oath, **Article Two, section one, last clause.**

When one reads our Constitution at Article two, section one, last clause it reads, ***"I do solemnly swear that I will faithfully execute the office of President of the United States and will to the best of my ability, preserve, protect and defend the Constitution of the United States of America.***

Bradly vs. Gay, Minn. NM 676 6,60   these Penial code at
241.1...*Gatewood v State 15 Md. App.341, 291A.2d, 551,553...*
***Vaughn v. State, 146 Tex. Cr.R 586,177 S.w.2d 59,60** and others*
***PERJURY – Title 1818 U.S.C. § sec.1622 (2012)** §1622.*
Subornation of perjury

That law specifies a convention call is peremptory on Congress
when the states have applied for a convention call and uses the
word shall to state this. The states have applied. When members of
Congress disobey the law of the Constitution and refuse to issue a
call for an Article V Convention when peremptorily required to do
so by that law, they have asserted a veto power when none exists
nor was ever intended to exist in that law. This veto alters the form
of our government by removing one of the methods of amendment
proposal the law of the Constitution creates. Such alteration
without amendment is a criminal violation of 5 U.S.C. 7311 and 18
U.S.C. 1918.

Second Accusation

***Whoever procures another to commit any perjury is guilty of
subornation of perjury, and shall be fined under this title or
imprisoned not more than five years, or both.***

***(June 25, 1948, ch. 645, 62 Stat. 774; Pub. L. 103–322, title
XXXIII, §330016(1)(I), Sept. cjs 13, 1994, 108 Stat. 2147.)***
We citizens should have pressured our people in Congress to
consider the point of removing him from office. At least an attempt
would have shown the world, especially our allies where this
republic stands and its policies coexist with them.

Third Accusation

Obama has failed to identify with the Constitution, acting as if a king

Moreover the Constitution reads at Article One, first section, *"All legislative Powers herein granted shall be vested in a Congress of the United States, which will consist of a Senate, House of Representatives."* Plus Article One sec.8, where we find *these powers are enumerated*, moreover the President is NEVER mentioned within this Article.

Again we find at Article One section eight, the *"Congress will make All Laws which shall be necessary and proper for carrying into execution the foregoing Powers, and all other Powers vested by this Constitution in the government of the United States, or in any department or Officer thereof."*
At *2 U.S.C.A. sec. 192 also sec.194 in accordance with U.S. Am 9-90 020 Definition.*

That law specifies a convention call is peremptory on Congress when the states have applied for a convention call and uses the word shall to state this. The states have applied. When members of Congress disobey the law of the Constitution and refuse to issue a call for an Article V Convention when peremptorily required to do so by that law, they have asserted a veto power when none exists nor was ever intended to exist in that law. This veto alters the form of our government by removing one of the methods of amendment proposal the law of the Constitution creates. Such alteration without amendment is a criminal violation of 5 U.S.C. 7311 and 18 U.S.C. 1918.

Congress has the authority to hold a person in contempt if the person's conduct or action obstructs the proceedings of Congress or, more usually, an inquiry by a committee of Congress.

U.S. law: Quinn v. U.S., 349 U.S. 155, 75 S. Ct. 668, 99 L. Ed. 964, 51 A.L.R.2d 1157 (1955).

Myers vs Stephens Cal. Repr. 420, 433, 233 C.A. 2d 104 ...As in fact it did result in the wrong, directly or proximately and without reference to the special character, condition, circumstances of we the plaintiffs.

Fourth Accusation

President Obama's willingness to defy Congress

Let's remember Nancy Pelosi words, "**We have to pass the (health care bill) so you can find out what is in it**".‗ So nobody read it and it passed and to this day not one of our leaders, knows what truly exist within it, including Nancy Pelosi. We are able to see what's in the title, **Patient Protection and Affordable Care Act and Other Things**. Clearly it is not about health care, rather insurance plans and what are the "Other Things"? Think about those words and refocus upon the words within this title, amazing how voluntary ill-equipped and essentially poorly informed "we the people" are concerning the activities within our government.

Refocusing on the charges against past President Obama, as with his willfulness changing *HR 3962 being a part of, at IRS CODE 1986* **Affordable Care Act.** This law became applicable on Jan. 1 2014. He, Obama defined the law and willfully and illegally granted to all corporations, with fifty or more full time employees an extension of the law for a period of one year. This violation is criminal on its face, an impeachable offence, described at **Article Two, section Two, fourth clause,** U.S. Constitution. **To confirm or to validate what was before void or unlawful. To add authority of law to that which was before unlawful or against the law... 126 N.J.L. 517, 27 A.2d709, 712**

Fifth Accusation .....Subsides to help persons unable to pay for The Affordable Care Act
A PART OF SECTION 1401 (Generally called subsides)
At (2), (A)

(1) IN GENERAL. The term 'premium *assistance* credit amount' means, with respect to any taxable year, the sum of the premium assistance amounts determined under paragraph with respect to all coverage months of the taxpayer occurring during the taxable year.

(1) PREMIUM ASSISTANCE AMOUNT A premium assistance amount determined under this subsection with respect to any coverage month is the amount equal to the lesser of—

(A) the monthly premiums for such month for 1 or more qualified health plans offered in the **individual market within a State** which cover the taxpayer, the taxpayer's spouse, or any dependent (as defined in section 152) of the taxpayer and which were enrolled in through an **Exchange established by the State** under 1311 of the Patient Protection and Affordable Care Act

(B) the excess (if any) of—

(1)(The adjusted monthly premium for such month for the applicable second lowest cost silver plan with respect to the taxpayer, over

(2) An amount equal to 1/12 of the product of the **Applicable Percentage** of the Tax payer's household income for the taxable year.

In my opinion this issue need not be heard by the Supreme Court, this law is so well defined there was no disputed case or scope for standing, purely clear and simple facts on their face value.

Once more deliberately and defiantly with wanton disregard of the law as written.

. Then again we have a law entitled "Legal Fraud", an act though not intended of actual evil design to perpetrate fraud, yet by their tendency to mislead others or to violate confidence, is prohibited by law. ... 61 Ohio App. 21,22, N.E.2d 293,297, 57 O. O. and Bartolucci v F alletti, 314 Ill. App. 551,4 N.E.2d 777, 780

This is still law and someone needs to exercise accordingly. Thus Mr. Obama apart and notwithstanding, accountable for his criminal actions under this appropriate stated law.

Sixth Accusation

Again President Obama's misuse of power defying the laws

U.S. SUPREME COURT at 259
U.S. 20 **Bailey vs. Drexel**
Furniture Co.
Decided May15, 1922... Syllabus

An act of Congress which clearly on its face, is designed to penalize, and hereby to discourage or suppress, conduct the regulation of which is reserved by the Constitution exclusively to the states, cannot be sustained under the federal taxing power by calling the penalty a tax, as appropriately explained previously. **P.259 U.S. 37, 533: McCray vs. UNITED STATES, 195 U.S.27; Flint vs. Stone Tracy Co., 220 U.S. 107** President Obama in violation of a legal instrument transposing a tax to punish, clearly designed for coercion by convoluting the word penalty into tax. The conflict involved is not problematic, it is again merely a misuse of the law as written in the Tenth

Amendment...*The powers not delegated to the United States by the Constitution, nor prohibited by it to the states are reserved respectively, or to the people.* As for past president ... *faithful execute the Office of the President of the United States, and will to the best of my ability, preserve, protect and defend the Constitution of the United States".*

We find that which a person bound to do, any duty imposed by law or promise **Rucks Brandt Const. Co. v Price Okl.165, 178, 23 and**

Helvering v British-American Tobacco Co C.C.A. 69F, 528, 530

I have carefully researched the origin of the phrase "high crimes and misdemeanors" and it's meaning to the Framers. I found the essential key understanding its true meaning is the word "high". It does not mean "more serious". It refers to those punishable offenses which *only apply to high persons, that is, to public officials, those who because of their official status, are under special obligations ".* Professor Roland

: **Intent to mislead.** The witness must know that the testimony is false and must give it with the intent to mislead the court. **Only false statements are perjury.** False testimony (willfully, knowingly) that results from testimony can be construed as perjury, if one of the conflicting statements is necessarily false and prosecutors can prove perjury without proving *which one* is false. **See Penal code at 241.1 ...and U.S 18 U.S.C.A. at 1642.** A person convicted of perjury under federal law may face up to five years in prison and fines. **Extrinsic fraud:** *Deception that is collateral to the issue being considered; intentional, maliciously misrepresentation outside the transaction itself, depriving one party or (groups of persons) of informed consent or full participation.* *C.S.J. sec. 309 at 375, 441, (1).* Moreover I believe Mr. Obama has no attachment to our republic, has broken his oath on numerous occasions, therefore willfully disregarded our laws, due to his thinking, laws are but a repugnancy. This only suggest that his intent to disregard the law, thus on its face is abhorrent and adverse. **Swan vs, The United States:** *contradiction in allegation of material facts.* *3 wyo.151,9 p931 and 27Am ju stat 110,41 p.l. at 47.* Furthermore in the *State v Moher 169 Wash.368, 13 p.2d 454, 455.* *A contemptuous opposition or utter disregard openly expressed, hence in words or action.*

Seventh Accusation

Past President Obama's procedures fly in the face of *14th Amendment*, *section 3 last half*, again his total and absolute defiance of any laws, he may find obstructive to his ideology, These laws have been devoured and destroyed left little if any ability for reasonable considerations.

Article Two sec. four, of these matters and brought by means of the Constitution's intention, where it enhances the essential need for Impeachment proceedings obvious.

I believe his deeds are treason, which are rendering the enemy aid and comfort.
The law is clear, see **18 U.S.C.A. at 2381 and Cramer v U.S., U.S.N.Y. 325 U.S. 1, 65, S. CT. accessibility**

Eighth Accusation

The fraud perpetrated upon the American people by past President Obama, were he lies and expounds so habitually, stating *"If you like your Doctor you can keep your Doctor, if you like your health plan, you can keep your health plan"* etc., this knowing full well he was lying, is called perjury, an instance of deliberately lying, making material false and /or misleading statements. *Case: **U.S. Criminal Justice System - perjury 1 sections 2-23, 5-8-21... also 18 U.S.C.A., 161 and 162, plus Gatewood v State 15 Md. App. 314, 2090 A. 2d 551, 553.***

Deception/fraud: fraud being an intentional perversion of truth, for the purpose of inducing another person in reliance upon it, to part with a valuable thing belonging to him, or to surrender legal rights.   **Johnson v McDonald... 170 Okl.117, 39 P2d, 150...** *plus* **Citizen Standard Life insurance. Gilly Tex. Civ. Civ.App521 S.W.2d 354,356.** *Deception; the act of intentional misleading by falsehoods spoken, are synonymous with fraud.* **Jackman vs. Mau at, 78 C. A. 234, 177 P. 2d 599, 605.** *Knowingly and willfully making a false statement pertaining to a present or past existing facts.* The intention of the person ought to be subservient to the law, not the law to the intention.

Noah Webster; perversion, *"one who is obstinate in the wrong, disposed to be contrary, distorted from the correct". Action ex delicto; an action arising from a breach of duty, coming from out of a contract.* **McCullough vs. the American workman: 200 S.C., 84, 20 S.E. 2d 640**

The accumulative action of deception, fraud and perversion are in fact treason, or of betraying the nation into the hands of a foreign power. Treason consisting of two elements. Adherence to the enemy and rendering him aid, abetting him and granting him comfort...***Cramer v* U.S. , US, N.Y.325 U.S,1, 65Ct. 918,932,89 L eD,1441 see U.S.C.A. at 2381**

Regardless Mr. Obama, shall it be fraud, deception or perversion? The protection of the two-witness rule of the Constitution in such a case extends at least to all acts of the defendant which are used to draw incriminating inferences that aid and comfort have been given. *P. 325 U. S. 33.* In a prosecution upon an indictment charging treason by adhering to enemies of the United States, giving them aid and comfort, in violation of *§ 1 of the Criminal Code two of the overt acts alleged and relied on were: P. 325 U. S. 34.*

Ninth Accusation Possibility of aiding and comforting the enemy

With respect to the unlawful Bowe Bergdahl exchange for five high level Taliban leaders, his flaunting of Bergdahl in front of the nation as a prize, was a disgrace. Had the President followed the simple requirement, one that **he** signed into law, following this need for responsibility, then many of the dangers posed by this decision could have been avoided altogether.

Hence as part of the, **H.R. 2397** *2014 National Defense Authorization Act and the Consolidated Appropriations Act of 2014,* he defied this Act, willfully and remains in violation thereof. However he, in his willful defiant attitude not having any respect for this law, again on the face of his refusal to conform is in non-compliance with *Maestas v. American Metal Co. of New Mexico 37 n.m. 203 20P.2d 924, 94 "Do not separate text from historical background. If you do, you will have perverted and subverted the Constitution, which can only end in a distorted, bastardized form".* James Madison.

Tenth Accusation

Now the five terrorists Obama released from Gitmo will in point, all return to the battle field and we the people were again deceived, what's more the deserter Bergdahl has finally been charged with desertion, not yet found guilty and obviously not sentenced.

It is not often that a soldier who deserted his post in the face of the enemy, has five Taliban Guantánamo detainees exchanged for his release from captivity, is welcomed back to the United States, and has Obama's national security adviser, Susan Rice praise him for having served his country "with honor and distinction." New York Times

Therefore, corresponding to this reason he be charged accordingly, by the Congress. Treason: *An act of attempting to over throw the government of a state to which one owes allegiance, which he is a part.* Now this matter becomes quite confusing. *[cases: treason C. J. S. 1, 2-3, 5]...* **U.S. Code › Title 18 › Part I › Chapter 115 › § 2381 See Article Three Sec. Three.** Only more of Mr. Obama's proceedings and his exploits against our people which are the principle of government, his intent to destroy our freedom, liberties and authority as individuals however he remains accountable.

Eleventh Accusation

Intrusion of our southern borders, failure to deal with this breach.

Our southern borders remain unprotected, yet our past President Obama has chosen to use a spurious, unconstitutional act to create a hoax played on millions of illegal immigrants. America shares 7,000 miles of land border with Canada and Mexico, as well as rivers, lakes and coastal waters around the country. These borders are economic gateways that account for trillions of dollars in trade and travel each year.

The Constitution clearly defines the responsibility of government to protect its citizens from dangers within and witho*ut: "Article* *four sec.4 The United States shall guarantee to every State in this Union a Republican Form of Government, and shall protect each of them against Invasion; and Application of the Legislature, or of the Executive (*when the Legislature cannot be convened*).*

Obviously President Obama has failed again to honor another segment of the Constitution. This obligation and the function of the House and Senate remains; "*an impeachable offense for the Commander in Chief to disobey this clear and unequivocal command of the U.S. Constitution.*" **See Chapter 8 U.S.C.A. 1101 (a) (15).** *The term 'immigrant' means every alien…This with the exception of an alien* who is *an ambassador, public minister, or career diplomatic.* May also be an alien other than one coming for the purpose of study or of performing skilled or unskilled labor or as a representative of foreign press, radio, film, or any other form of foreign information.

"Furthermore, an illegal immigrant is a criminal in three circumstances, as *in chapter 8 U.S.C.A.* **at SECTION 1325, ONE,** enters *at the wrong time or place,* ***TWO****, eludes examination by immigration officers, or* ***THREE****, obtains entry by fraud".* Which this illegal **per se**, unlawful in and of itself, and not because of some extraneous circumstance. ***Schmitt v. Wright, 317 Ill. App. 384, 48N.E.2d 184, 192*** *and* ***Natural soda co. v. city of Los Angeles Cal App, 132, P. 2d 553,563.***

Perhaps this would better be stated, if we could, simply impeach him, as this would have prevented further destruction of our republic and our Constitution.

The constant referral to Article Two sec. four was the necessary action at the time of his actual infringement of our Constitution. I feel a need to justify myself for the congresses failure to act upon his miscarriage, that being for not fulfilling his duty as president.

Twelfth Accusation

Benghazi events exist today as before, Mr. Obama as with Mrs. Clinton ... Treason

The President stated an anti-Muslim tape made by an American, generated the attack in Benghazi, knowingly he spoke with mendacity, contending that the taped video gave impetus for the attack, which knowingly was deliberately and falsely indicated, as they knew it was an act of terrorism. *U.S.C.A. Title 18 at 2381, plus Article lll sec lll U.S. CONSTITUTION*

As Chief Executive of our republic, he was the representative of our people and is morally obligated to act thusly. He knowingly, willfully and intentionally lied to the love ones of these fallen heroes, defying the law and morality. As stated before, all laws broken, (parted by violence through word or action) by anyone including the President, is at least a misdemeanor or at least should be treated as such an impeachable offence. Again he is still accountable criminally. *Gatewood vs. state, 15 MD 314, 290A.2d 551,553 Since perjury is a crime when a lawful oath is administered to a person who swears willfully and absolutely falsely, in a matter material to an issue, point in question, If he believes it not to be true.... Subornation of perjury is procuring another to commit perjury. 18 USCA at 1622.*

The preceding pages may appear protracted, instead for the crimes he commited they are short and the charges are many and could have been more serious. Plus the list of crimes far more numerous.

Chapter Nine

Our Republic regarding race relations and its many disturbances creating considerable instabilities.

The deaths of Michael Brown and Eric Garner were the perfect events for the experience of the "Saul Alinsky style community organizers", exploiting these activities for use to incite, therefore affecting a market for and about their agenda. This criminal alliance is dedicated to the destruction of civil order and the rule of law within the cities of America. Notwithstanding, I remain optimistic there may still be time to defeat this tide of evil facing our republic, if our society turns to God and executes His precepts and put into action the visions of our founders. There may still be time, however the moment has cast its authoritative spirit upon us, a beneficial assignment of action and we by necessity, are required to move quickly in order to halt the flood of these criminal proceedings which draws closer each day. Therefore as for myself, I imagine sentiment set in motion by necessary measures, is quickly parting, leaving me without the words to properly express the urgency for which the task ahead requires.

God will not fail in His promise to guide and support, **Numbers 13 verses 31, 32,** the Israelites failed to trust God in their oncoming battle, they believed victory was impossible, failing to remember God does not operate from a human prospective, a promise from God is an indubitable thing. Are we willing to stand against the pressures of prevalent opinion and follow His perceptions? Even so, it requires we begin to move, as a vehicle cannot turn directions unless it's moving, we are obliged to be in motion in order to receive God's assistance and trying to obey His design for our society. I realize the Democrats have become more and more socialistic and intend to advance their manifesto of Saul Alinsky and his platform "Rule for Radicals" or Obama's "Rules for Revolution".

However I'm concerned the clergy arrives on the scene weak and a bit late, reluctant to lead the people due to the infamous law instigated by President Johnson some sixty years ago, the **IRS code...501(c) 3.** This law suggest that clergy and the church shall not indulge *"in no part of the net earnings of which familiarizes to the benefit of any private shareholder or individual, no substantial part of the activities of which is carrying on propaganda, or otherwise attempting, to influence legislation (except as otherwise provided in subsection (h)), and which does not participate in, or intervene in (including the publishing or distributing of statements), any political campaign on behalf of (or in opposition to) any candidate for public office", (sub-section H has little or no relationship to this issue*). Of course the Constitution prohibits such action on the part of the government. The above is part of the IRS Code having no authority relevant to this matter. The leaders of Christian churches and groups have an obligation to rearrange this spurious law or have it rescinded, or at least give it any consideration whatsoever, as the law was written by a counterfeit President (Johnson) by name, through a deceptive method. If there is to be any change in our republic's direction, it's the clergy that ought to spearhead the change and be the impetus, the precursor generating the necessary enthusiasm, causing their church people to admire and respect them.

I do believe if this were to happen many people would be converted, Christians along with a number of whom are on the verge, will justifiably edge away from our flawed secular politicians, whom care little if any of Christianity. Their experience without backbone, a change could come about due to any reasonable thinking, for the so called conservative party. The "GOP" now having control of the House and Senate, seems merely a dream. I consider both parties are all about themselves with little if any concern for their constituents, the citizens that hired and positioned them to representing and serve, along with others in Washington D.C. When one looks at the ideology of these two parties we find the Democrats saying their goal is to help working and poor folks through free food, housing, health care and even cell phones.

 There's no such things or objects being free, only simple "showcases", someone else is paying, we tax payers. My designation for these many programs are "handouts", while there are some folks requiring help, most are simply lazy deadbeats, unwilling to work and have never understood the basic inner demand for work. It persists without a doubt, whereas our clergy and the church has failed miserly, both decisively and most profoundly. Therefore, ultimately leaving a vacuum which government was more than delighted to fill, with your money, called taxes.

 Republicans on the other hand have chosen to be all things to all people, passing on their agenda with nothing but empty words. I regard their willingness to return to God's standards, as pure propaganda for our consumption and that sorry rhetoric did not originate with our founders, simply pure rhetoric, devoid of any lack of significance. Furthermore, they propose doing more with less by cutting waste and corruption in government, now this is where I have attempted humor. If anything they have become the essence of squander, waste and corruption, furthermore warriors attempting to implement our ideals through force rather than example. They coexists as both parties subsists having aspirations of larger government thus having more dominance over our lives and the future lives of our children and their children.

The Congress being in control of the budget, are now more than ever capable and responsible, as a consequence should decide what needs to be spent on obligations, those needed to operate according to the Constitution, as enumerated in "Article One sec. eight", of course the politicians have long destroyed the provisions therein, now it's the needs of our national governmental growth, creating provisions and operations which failed. There is however no need for concern, as they only spend our money, the Ninth and Tenth amendments exists for reasons such as these, projects best designed and controlled by the states, when managed correctly, our taxes would decrease dramatically. This sequence is but a dream, rather from the very beginning the founders proposed with the intention of a two party system, the idea being to debate different points of view coming from various areas of the union. Now they only argue for the exclusive purpose of gaining power, influence and money from the citizens, taxes, it's quite difficult to ascertain and judge which party to place our trust, when both are corrupt, they are both habitually non- compliant with the Constitution, consequently all their jabbering by no means, distinguishing one from another.

At this point with respect to the illegal protesting, generally the Afro-Americans are missing the foundation of our legal system, one could clearly see while in their haste to judgment, people such as Al Sharpton have deceived them for his own personal gain and future. As little expertise, rather a hatred of what they perceive to be fact, that white people have perpetrated this act upon them, while this may be true in a few cases, as their own people in many cases have sworn quite the opposite picture. Nevertheless, believing this grants them a justification to vent, which is a good thing, when exercised properly. These people are driven by the media and agitators much reminiscent of Jesse Jackson and Ben Jealous, Black panthers, among others. Then we have Al Sharpton in a category by himself and one of his own making, nothing more than a low life criminal, moreover failing to pay his federal taxes, to the tune of one and half million dollars, there is nothing reverent about him.

This attitude once again demonstrates that distrust in law enforcement presents a grave danger to our civil fabric, this I regard as the moral responsibility of our elected officals. This to clear the air of mistrust, since it is they are the ones who caused this complex issue to occur in the first place. A police force is an established body of persons empowered by the state under oath, to enforce the law, protect person, property and keep a tight rein on civil disorder. I am reasonably confident few of our citizens comprehend or appreciate the meaning of the Fifth Amendment, therefore missing the point of this essential and fundamental provision, regrettably lacking this knowledge. This critical dilemma clearly creates a problematic condition, to whom do we owe our allegiance, the protesters that seem ignorant of the law, the police or the grand jury, or most of all the agitators, which includes President Obama. This question needs to be answered in the hearts of all citizens.

My reading of the Fifth Amendment which defines beyond a doubt, "unless on a presentment or indictment of a grand jury", this seems to embrace all questions with regards to the issue at hand. Now what is troubling for me, since past President Obama and Eric Holder are both lawyers, why did they persist in being agitators and openly defying the law and defending the protesting individuals? People who falsely imagine concepts and notions, which they believe in someway their actions become rights granted by the Constitution.

In defense of my past words being too strong, read this written by an Afro- American woman; in two separate videos uploaded to YouTube Monday, this unnamed woman posting under the username "Honestly Speaking" unleashed a tirade against Al Sharpton, calling him a **"disgusting disgrace to humanity"** and decrying the civil rights leader as a **"race-baiting, tired, pathetic ... no good for nobody a**.** The woman started her fiery rebuke with a 50-second clip railing against Sharpton's recent revelation that he received death threats in the wake of the murders of NYPD Officers Rafael Ramos and Wenjian Liu.

"Leave it to Reverend Al Sharpton to make two cops having been murdered about him. Nobody cares that you received death threats. Nobody cares about you. You are the reason this is happening," she proclaimed. "Take your old, stale, trouble-making, race-baiting, tired, pathetic, perverted, coke-sniffing no good for nobody a** go somewhere and sit down."

As for De Blasio, she delivered a similar message. "De Blasio, Mike Brown is not your son".

"You have been brainwashed into believing in a super duper space daddy or mommy, by bronze age goat herders". Your religion is not even original, your savior, is based on another so called messiah who existed centuries before yours came into being. Like I said, keep venerating your genocidal, child murdering deity, ignorance is bliss, and you are a most happy fellow".

 As for Christianity, attacked along with many others things, against such as Catholicism globally, including the United States, is becoming stronger, while devoid of, or little resistance from Christians and their leaders. I firmly believe as a nation we are becoming more and more secular and socialist, yielding a significant amount of faith in government rather than faith in God, the God our founders were so infected with, trusting God for strength and wisdom.   This present hour demands resuming the specifics of our political leaders and our churches along with the clergy, restoring the extremely basic ideals which founded this republic, without which we are doomed. While some speak of a wall between religious activities and government, I find in the First Amendment that "government must refrain from establishing a religion, or prohibiting the free exercise thereof". Their fear and concern came from the past, the British imposing their demands about this regard. However if a **wall** exist, it in no way ever suggest religious pursuits to intervene in governments affairs, nor in any way suggest it be restricted.

Another issue which occurs while referring to the attack on Christianity, is the issue of free speech. It appears the attack on both these subjects stem from our First Amendment, as both of these principles work hand in hand and the persons writing them placed them at the top of their agenda. This stipulates to me, the importance they assigned to the two questions we are speaking of and their laying them out in words of very unambiguous English.

While I may give the impression that all is lost, sandwiched on the other hand, while it's true we are on the brink of disaster there is still time for change. As we have been provided a power from God and the willing to go down a course of profoundly new but difficult choices. Since our society has elected a complex route, the results have left us in an inferior situation with inadequate options. Thus we ought to move ahead and expand our adaptations, we should act against challenges that may create setbacks and problems for individuals and our society. Yet there are essential goals, dedications and purposes which we must aspire, creating better lives. As God is our source of power we are capable of these goals, if with determination we seek His direction.

The first point, maintain and be consistent, while being firm with our politicians, to induce suggestions, coordinate and/or orchestrate the many bureaucratic departments, then disband the Federal Reserve, go back to the Constitution. Then remove our illegal tax code and in the process the I.R.S. which would no longer survive, therefore relish in its departure, as the billions saved would go to worthwhile issues and perhaps lower taxes. In what way may I ask, have citizens taken into account that for more than 125 years our national government stood and progressed without "income tax". Our Constitution clearly defines the obligation which they are expressly duty-bound to defend. During those years all these obligations were fulfilled, the Congress never gave the people an impression of a great need for large additional funds, or being allegedly needed or presumably considered necessary.

Nevertheless, in 1913 Congress defended a need for a small tax on large corporations and industry, this tax to be laid on their income from "whatever source derived and without apportionment among the several states"… This sounds to me as an indirect tax which was already in existence, as in 1913 the Supreme Court stated "no new tax had been written since the Congress already had the power to lay and collect taxes". For me it's the confusion in which the wording presents some questions, such as the word **income,** nevertheless, making it a direct tax.

Examining Noah Webster dictionary we see his definition, "that **gain** which proceeds from, business, property etc. and/or applied to the **gain** of private persons". In Ballantine's law dictionary we find, "for tax purpose the gain derived from capital, labor or both combined." Again in Noah Webster dictionary the word most often used, gain, is defined as "profit, increase or interest, to obtain by industry or the employment of capital, to acquire as **profit**".

Nevertheless, perhaps it's more appropriate that I answer this question, explaining the main reason why again our Supreme Court perverted our Constitution and lied to the American people. Within our Constitution at Article One, sec.8 the limited powers to tax are enumerated for the national government, all else are reserved rights to the states. This, for what reason or purpose is there to enumerate if a general power, could eclipse them. These are the rights bestowed to the states and or enumerated in our Constitution. Let us remember, the unification of the states was to *"form a more perfect union"* between one another. However, they would never ever give up their sovereignty, as each and every state had and has its own Constitution and government.

The Supreme Court invalidated state laws by prohibiting or restrictions, which lacks any basis in the text, since logic, structure or original understanding of the Constitution, must prevail. **In *U.S. vs Butler 1936*** an earlier Roberts, wrote, "*...this tax invades the reserved rights of the states. Therefore a matter beyond the powers delegated to the federal government, the tax is but a means to an unconstitutional end*".

The misuse of words which fell completely within the Affordable Care Act, where John Roberts stunned and annihilated many Americans reversing the word penalty into tax. When checking, I never found these words synonyms or an alternative word to be used for an alternative expression, never. We find neither did Justice **Antonin Scalia,** challenging Justice Roberts who lost without an answer.

The essence of my point stands on the fact the average American citizen works and is paid in exchange for his labor, where is the gain derived, there is no gain, no increase or profit, only an exchange of earnings for labor, the earnings being equal to labor. Once more our government deceived the American people, this was sold on the idea the general public as a whole would not be taxed. Trying not to get into the weeds too far, the reason government used **indirect** taxation, as they chose to claim it was, rather than **direct,** which it was, as direct taxes would be utterly obvious and in all probability rejected. The concept of more taxes would be proper to meet the needs of a growing Republic were necessary to address in *Article one sec. 2, third clause, so it was.*

However to this day that tax, a direct tax controlled and laid and agreed upon the individual soveriegn states, has never been approached as it's so simple the national government has not been capable to envision a way for cheating, or swindling the public. This tax is applied to each state individually according to its respective population, and their Representatives. However, (the persons bound to servitude and Indians not taxed three fifths etc.), has been resolved in the fourteenth Amendment and therefore each state is obliged to collect the necessary funds from their citizen by whatever means the citizens elect. Thus creating more questions about these taxes, asking are these additional funds needed, remember as equal representation of sovereign states.

This is exactly why our Founders gave notice to King George of England, "taxation without representation won't get it". So a rebellious group of upstarts began a war only believing God would support their efforts. Read Patrick Henry's speech at the Virginia colonies delegation, called the ": give me liberty or give me death".

Why do we *pay **income tax?, ignorance,*** when our early congress knew that in time there would be a need for additional funds, to support the efforts of the national political body and provide the needs for a growing nation. You shall find in Article one, section 2, clause 3, read it for yourself, as I have claimed.

I certainly understand why we need more funds, as the Constitutional requirements grow, so grows our national government's needs grow to fulfill their accountability, and Article 1. sec. 2. Clause 3. , satisfies and accomplish this concern. The obstruction came from the government its self, their control would be entrusted to the scrutiny of the states, each sovereign state legislator judging and reporting to the people to what particular extent necessary and how this tax would be collected. Let's not forget this tax was collected once every ten years, "unless in such manner as they by law may determine". Having a bit of fun, by need the timing and progression would of course be tailored to the necessary requirements.

Once again I will turn to Blacks law, there we find that "Income Tax" *endures a tax on the yearly profits arising from property, business pursuits, professions, trades, or offices, etc.* A tax levied by government whether federal or state.

Once more, *the gain derived from capital, the return in money from one's business, labor or effort, thus including profit or gain through sale of conversion of capital. The true increase of wealth which comes to a person during a stated period of time.* **Goodrich vs Edwards 255, U.S.527, S, Ct, 390, 65, L, ED 758**

We take a peek at GAIN in yet again Blacks law. *Gain Profits, Winnings, increase in value, difference in value between receipts and expenditures then financial gain.* On and on we read these words, profits, gains, increase. **C.C.A. 10, 43 F 2d, 327, 328 Gain is the profit**

Under federal tax law this is either the gross income of the business or the adjusted gross income, of both either business or individuals. It is the **accrual** of some profit, gain, or benefit. The word gain: Gain is the profit derived from capital or something of exchangeable value, drawn from capital by an individual for his separate use. **Internal Revenue vs Simmons Gin Co. C.C.A. 10, 43 F 2d, 327, 328 Gain is the profit**

It is my opinion and desire to ask the question, where is **my gain, increase, or profit,** I am devoid of such, as are you?

I am essentially certain no employer, small or large expects you to gain, increase, or profit a greater wealth from your work, only the exchange of so much work, for significant funds to support what your needs may require and remembering those words. Life, Liberty and the Pursuit of Happiness. Fraud in law **Definition:** *fraud that is presumed to have occurred in light of the circumstances irrespective of intent to deceive.*

I solicit your observation. Fact: It remains my conviction and pure denunciation, as the entire matter of Income Tax is fraud. **Fraud in law**; description in Black's law Dictionary stands with this, *fraud in the contemplation of law, fraud implied or inferred by law, fraud made out by construction of law.* Please tell me, if this is not fraud commited through **income tax, the IRS and our**

government. While the congress of the United States fully created and supported this situation.

So once again government crept and inched the idea forward of one percent at a time and until WW2 came the payroll tax (actually still income tax) to support the war effort, who could use rates that have risen and fallen over the last seventy years. This depending upon the idiocy of the people we hired to represent our interest. The cost to support their programs, which unelected bureaucrats are hired to administer and manipulate, are some triggers which caused taxes to escalate. The obvious alternative remains less regulations and more freedom, till the national government severely reduces their control, rather having the state governments define and determine the needs of the people in each particular state, as spelled out, reading for all in the Ninth and Tenth Amendments.

All sovereignty and power not enumerated in the Constitution *shall be reserved to the states respectively, nor shall the enumerated rights in the Constitution be denied or disparage others retained by the people.*

So why have we allowed individuals in Washington D.C. to grow disgustingly and repulsively without restraint, there needs to be some form of true limitation on the scope of their prolonged endeavors, after they take an oath of office. As this is a position they never-endingly begged on behalf of, spending million upon millions, why then ought one to believe their motives. They have only proven to be deceptive and untrue, only game players.

Where does a large chunk of your wasted tax dollars disappear?

Looking at the history of our congress and the staff they employ, due to pathetic building and creäting public industries and many, many unnecessary programs and departments.

Before the **Civil War**, members of Congress did not have staff assistance or even offices, while most simply worked at their personal desks. Then some years later, in 1891, Congress had a total of 146 staff members: 37 Senate personal staff, 39 Senate committee staff, and 62 House committee staff (37 of whom only worked during congressional sessions). The House had approved personal staff for Representatives in 1893.- Now since the beginning of the 20th century, congressional staff had become a well-accepted feature of congressional operations. The national government began growing before the turn of the century, one can wonder why in 1913 congress passed the income tax fraud upon the American public, accordingly they flourished and grew faster and faster.

In 1943, House committees employed 114 staff members, while Senate committees employed 190 staff members. The size of individual members' personal staffs were still relatively small, with the average senator having six staffers and representatives limited to having five staffers. In the Legislative Reorganization Act of 1946, which reformed Congress and reduced the number of Congressional committees, then expressly authorized permanent, professional committee staff for the first time. The act provided for a much-needed increase in committee staff, allowing for up to four professional and six clerical staff members for each standing committee, except for the appropriations committees. Instead no limitation on the number of staff members. The 1946 act also reorganized the Library of Congress and created the Legislative Reference Service, which soon became the Congressional Research Service. The size of both personal and committee staff increased considerably after the passage of the Legislative Reorganization, following the significant increase in 1947. Think of what they had accomplished In only 34 years with our new tax money, they grow like weeds, is there no end to their personal achievements. Oh yes there was only gradual growth in the number of both kinds of staff for about twenty years. Increased staff specialization also occurred during this period of slow growth i.e., staffers began to be divided into press, legislative, and caseworker.

Above all congress is under a compulsion to continue to grow and has grown more corrupt, as citizens we are in need of guidance and for influence for our thinking, our faith. We the people need Gods care and protection, instruction on how we should live. Then help with education as every child is indeed of need, all these and others must be from the Bible and the Constitution, yet I fail to find any such ideology.

The above is pure love, as we need a bit of absurdity and our Congress is sure to provide. Let's not forget the Mid-East and the cost thereof plus problems we created with the Muslims more than fifty years ago. Sunni, Shiite and Kurds have been at war for over thousands of years, but we decided to have them become one nation, Iraq, then how well or in what way has this gone? Then with a democratic government, which much earlier was known as Babylonia, with many caliphate in the last two millenniums. They have forgotten Iran their antagonist, now wishing to acquire them? Our Congress has achieved their endeavors famously, implemented and accomplished so huge an achievement, with great distribution, but for whom? I see nothing for you and I the working citizens, only those politicians flippant with everything, while as always moving at a snail's pace. These servants we elected, who begged to serve, have created little else but chaos.

Returning to the 1970s, there was again a sharp jump in the number of staffers. This was a response "in part to increased workloads" workloads on whom and for what reason? Also in part for confrontation with the executive branch on various issues, including the past president's impoundment of funds and the **Watergate debacle.** Political scientist Morris P. Fiorina, in his book Congress: Keystone of the *Washington Establishment*, found that the number of congressional staff more than doubled between 1960 and 1974.

Today each congressperson is allotted up to $ 944,671.00 depending on the population of the state. Nearly 2,000 members of the House of Representatives staffers pulled down six-figure salaries in 2009, including 43 staffers who earned the maximum $172,500 or more than three times the median U.S. household income. Please, how has this become real. But while these top earners are a small percentage of the overall congressional work force, their numbers are growing at a rapid rate. The number of staffers earning within the upper 3 percent of House salaries is currently $163,358, plus more have increased by nearly 39 percent in the past four years, according to LegiStorm data. …*"These are people who could be making a lot more money in the private sector, but they choose to work here,"* said a Pelosi spokesman Brendan Daly, who also makes $172,500. These are true patriots, sacrificing so much for the country, a nation so so in need of them and their overwhelming skilled services, in fact there should be twice as many such overpaid persons, sorry I really meant underpaid highly skilled individuals.. … How could we have achieved such extreme chaos, through their lack of stupidity and incompetence? Today we have approximately 10,000 House staffers, including district office workers, according to the administrative officer.

Therefore, if after reading this data gives any indication for Congress to tackle this need, followed then by addressing the income tax fraud of Feb. 3rd 1913 and during the same year on Dec. 23rd 1913 of forming the Federal Reserve System. One may ask, why the Federal Reserve and I will give the answer.

The Federal Reserve Act, signed into law by President Woodrow Wilson, (a raving socialist) gave to 12 Federal Reserve Banks the ability to print money in order to ensure economic stability.

I find the Constitution requires the congress to implement this matter, Article one, section 8, clause 5 in the enumerated detail of their responsibilities. More specifically, the Federal Reserve System created and intended for a dual mandate, one, to maximize employment and two, keep inflation low.

However within a mere sixteen years our Republic was in the greatest depression and unemployment ran rampant, thus President Wilson and his idea for the Federal Reserve was transformed into an abject failure.

Nevertheless, we still suffer with that ideology along with Federal Income tax, a must for our national government. This though the national government would rather be called Federal. I have looked and was unable to find national or federal government only *we the people in order to form a more perfect union* no federal nor national government. Though in Article seven it pronounces *upon* ratification, *the Constitution was then established **between** the states*, nothing suggesting a national or federal government. Furthermore, over and over constantly I came across the words **The United States,** only once was there any connection, *a district ten sq. miles by the acceptance of Congress become the seat of the government of the United States.*

A few Responses from Individuals:

"When my bank wanted to make more loans to businesses in the area, we weren't able to do so because the Federal Reserve System had decided to lower the amount of money in the country and was refusing to lend us any money."

"I wanted to work in the Federal Reserve System because I had always loovved banks for all of my life and wanted to work in one."

"The people were all furious with the way their finances had been handled, but the banker assured them that it was not his fault but the Federal Reserve System

"Banks are not members of the <u>Federal Reserve System</u>."

In most respects it has failed, after fourteen changes by acts of Congress have ensued and failed, it has yet to secure our economy by control of inflation, nor have they maintained a steady, level platform for the working people of our Republic. The "great depression" began some sixteen years after its inception, the Federal Reserve has yet to put together a small number of workable concepts. While more than one hundred years have passed, they have simply not accomplished their supposed agenda. Still some did receive benefits, but most of us are not of that financial, elitist position.

It's time to move to our election, as established by the Constitution! We have a two party system, again devised by the founders of this our Republic. The idea was to have a conveyance of viewpoints, involving the submitting of political thinking, therefore gaining the knowledge of one another, after many hard exchanging of words.

Nevertheless, both parties gained new ideas from the other, assumed after wide-ranging passage of words. This was the manner in which our Republic was designed to perform, rather today we find they prefer to fight one another, war like and have strayed from the original concept.

The next on our intended litany of events is the 2016 election and the wild happenings thereof, along with the final two despicable individuals to face off with each other. I do believe this is a practical and a working manner for operating government.

Plus before closing one last accounting of the reporter Todd Starnes who's prayer I spoke of. In the Dec. 25 story "**VA hospital bans Christmas cards**," Starnes wrote that "bedridden veterans at the VA hospital" had been denied receiving Christmas cards written by elementary school students because the letters "violated VA policy."

Of Starnes' story, the VA explained its policy in this statement:

"In order to be respectful of our veterans' religious beliefs, all donated holiday cards are reviewed by a multi-disciplinary team of staff led by chaplaincy services and determined if they are appropriate (non-religious) to freely distribute to patients. We regret this process was not fully explained to this group and apologize for any misunderstanding."

As for myself, I clearly understand this is a wretched story and merely another example of how our government maintains its attitude toward Christians. There is no Christmas without the birth of Jesus Christ, how then were these elementary school children to send a Christmas card (a very beautiful idea) to adult military men and women. A picture of a snowman or Santa Claus, merry bells etc. This event is an extremely heartbreaking experience.

I have faith that Christian people will come to their senses and show responsibility, beginning to fight against this prosecution of our faith in God and His Son Jesus Christ.
Then as we take steps in this direction God will aid our effort and our efforts will come to fruition, since He will always succeed in His support for His people.
If we achieve in this activity it shall grant the determination needed for greater self-determination in our Republic and its citizens. The politics in Congress ought to follow the lead of those who have chosen to lead our Republic back to the ideals from whence it came and once again we shall be given the blessing of God.

Grove City College Students, Faculty, Riled by Pending Mike Pence. NFL Star Chris Maragos Says Mothers Considering Abortion 'Need Jesus' and Terrifying Twitter Freaks Out Over Marco Rubio Posting Bible Quotes.

All this on the loss of Christian ideals while nonetheless some realize and feel some of these ideas still remain. As I have stated above, we Christians have the largest share of the responsibility to press our leaders into refocusing their attention on their constituants and less time focused on the next election.
Now we need to move forward facing the Election of 2016 and all the nastiness it brought our nation.

Chapter Ten

The Chaotic and Tumultuous Election of 2016

My desire is for your to envisage a glimpse of our union of states which produced an original concept of governing, called a Republic. Thus led, possessed and controlled by the people. Having faith that my dissertation exhibited a depiction of our history, beginning before the Revolutionary War till today, some 325 years later. Though it was merely a snapshot of the many changes in the people, and how we chose to permit all three branches of government removing freedom from all focal points and the very breathes of our lives. Our Republic sadly became inoperative after we surrendered the original concepts and principles plus the majority have forgotten the God of our founders and the ideology He laid down for us to accept, His promise of "certain unalienable rights".

Still applicable is the mark of character to the idea we need to pledge to each other our lives, our fortunes and our sacred honour. In other words find unity and self- respect along with self- reliance. Driving toward that goal will diminish the drive and size of government, which should be our goal. In my life time, rarely have I seen the national government perform satisfactory, at its best, mediocrity, rather in all likelihood, primarily totally inept. I have looked but found nowhere in the Constitution the words *national government,* only- *upon ratification, the Constitution was then established between the states,* and *a district ten sq. miles by the acceptance of Congress become the seat of the government of the United States,* never Capitol, only the States were comprised of Capitols.

As I write regarding the infidelity of Barrack Obama's behavior as President of our Republic, our nation is embarking upon an election, most importantly that of President. Now choosing a person to lead our Republic, comprises additional importance and magnitude than ever. Though in this present year our process of selecting delegates leading to the choice for a candidate from either party, we have scrabbled beyond a doubt, yet we missed the mark completely. However the people through our system of choice, selecting particular individuals, thus we the people have spoken. Therefore bringing into view two major unfathomable participants. One from the Clinton crime family, or else recognized as Hillary Clinton, known best as lying Hillary Clinton, now engaged in an outrageously bizarre contest, all the while captivated and enthralled with the thought of being crowned, queen of the U.S.A.

Considering the other chosen participant, well known for his bombastic attitude toward life, a business man driven by duplicity and prone to outlandish operations, a thin skinned revengeful, lying individual. I feel there is little else to describe his persona. I have chosen to begin my facts and judgements with Hillary Clinton, an unscrupulous, corrupt individual and whose lifelong objectives were designed for and focused upon politics, one which she would never ever escape.

Presenting her political life needs to be studied then stated and presented in chronological order. This should be approached in an enumerated and documented structure, a summary of how she, Hillary Clinton spent forty five years of her adult life as desires of the political life, chiefly as to become President.

We begin with Hillary Rodham as a student at Wellesley College, an all- women's school and Alan Schechter, former Chairman of the Fulbright Foreign Scholarship Board, was a mentor to Hillary

Rodham.   Furthermore he was Professor of Political Science and was educated at Amherst College where he received his AB. He was also Hillary Rodham's political advisor during her years at college and supervised her senior thesis. Susan Estrich also recalls her writings pertaining to an honors thesis for the Professor. He remained involved with the college, running the Wellesley internship program at Washington D.C., in which Rodham participated as a student and which continues to send approximately twenty women to Washington for internships each summer.

 While at Wellesley she wrote, *"A Radical is one who advocates sweeping changes in existing laws and methods for government. Those proposed changes were aimed at the roots of political problems which in Marxian terms are the attitudes and behaviors of men."* Furthermore, Hillary's future willingness to tolerate Bill's compulsive philandering is a function of her general contempt for men. Again, at her graduation she wrote. *"My senior year at Wellesley would further test and articulate my beliefs. For my thesis I analyzed the work of a Chicago native and community organizer named Saul Alinsky".*

 Fact, he Saul Alinsky was the writer and ideologist for "Rules for Radicals" an extreme philosophy on politics and governing society. We must not forget, as a young man he was a member of the Al Capone Mob, but left as Scarface Al Capone's motives and interest were far different than Saul Alinsky. As stated above he wished to control people and their thinking of politics, Scarface cared nothing of their thinking, only money. My own judgement tells me, with regards for a foundation in life, Hillary's seems to be dependent and fixed on a heavily radical position, not designed or acceptable to a normal human nor any idea of such existing within them.

The early years of young Hillary Rodham's life while attending law school, is where and when she met Bill Clinton. The two dated for some time and together continued on serious political endeavours.

   As a young staff attorney she worked for the Judiciary Committee during the Watergate investigation. However she Hillary was fired by her supervisor, Jerry Eifman. When asked why she was fired, Eifman said in an interview, (by several news media), *"Because she was a liar. She was an unethical, dishonest lawyer, she conspired to violate the Constitution, the rules of the House, the rules of the Committee, and the rules of confidentiality."* Though Eifman, who now is retired, the general counsel and chief of staff for the House Judiciary Committee, was her director. Hillary while working on the Watergate investigation, she was known for her history of lies and unethical behaviour which goes back farther and goes much deeper than anyone realizes.

A few years later after Bill Clinton met Hillary at law school, they both moved to Arkansas where they were married on October 11, 1975, in the living room of their home in Fayetteville, Arkansas.

   At one point Bill and Hillary campaigned for Senator Fulbright. The same man who was an avid Klan's member, a vocally open supporter of segregation, and was 100% against the civil rights movement, who else was he? Beginning in 1976 a mentor to Bill and Hillary Clinton, thus fittingly it evolved, therefore he became Senator from Arkansas. Thus soon advocated and supported Bill Clinton for the office of Attorney General in 1976. Equally Senator Fulbright continued to support Clinton in his campaign for Governor of Arkansas in 1979 and 1983. During this time Hillary was hiding in Bill's shadow working with the Rose Law firm. Though not quite working for them only, she was part of the super-secretive committee on "Hillary-care" program. Vince Foster was a partner in the Rose law firm where Hillary was an attorney, at this point becoming good friends. Later he was Deputy White House Counsel during the first half-year of President Bill Clinton's administration. His death soon became quite controversial, however, being settled upon suicide, as the Clinton crime family was off to a great start moving forward.

Most Americans have forgotten, but in the 1990s, Hillary Clinton gained notoriety for initially being the only First Lady in American history, who was actually called to testify in front of a grand jury. Hillary was soon to become the individual who became the subject of the accusations. These activities of suspicious endeavours were concerning missing subpoenaed records from the Rose Law Firm. Of interest to prosecutors were the records from the White-water land deal in Arkansas and Hillary's legal representation for then convicted felon **Jim McDougal'**s savings and loan association, Madison Guaranty. Meanwhile remember it is hardly Hillary Clinton's first rodeo when it comes to document destruction. Whether it was the Rose Law Firm, or the firing of the White House travel office, all the while she remained unaffected.

Meanwhile the story of her lost records, as non-emergence of these records was a matter of procedure, these were the Madison Guaranty records. This in time for the Congressional enquiry, plus into her many problems with the Rose firm. With only denial for explanation provided by Hillary, "I have absolutely no idea where these documents, the subpoenaed documents could have gone. Then these same documents turned out to have been in her custody the entire time, investigators called in the Federal Bureau of Investigation to "ascertain Hillary's role in their mysterious disappearance." An FBI fingerprint analysis concerning the Rose Law Firm billing records, revealed there were two significant sets of fingerprints on the missing subpoena documents, those of White House Deputy Legal Counsel Vince Foster and Hillary Clinton. Of course Vince Foster was found dead. These documents were never surrendered, nor did they appear before the congressional committee.

Nevertheless a housekeeper of Hillary's came across them in an up- stairs bedroom-office by accident while cleaning and realized the importance to the existence of these documents, thus turning them over to authorities. Hillary Clinton herself, of course stated she had "no idea" how the documents had ended up there, this is just another of Hillary's unquestionable lie.

In the midst of the investigation, Foster died in what was ruled a self-inflicted gunshot wound, however then indeed more deception emerged. A hard drive from Foster's White House computer went missing. It eventually turned up in the Old Executive Office Building across the street from the White House, but investigators ultimately were unable to recover or provide evidence from the hard drive, for reason it had been purposely and significantly damaged. Autopsy photos of Vince Foster will never be released.

Furthermore, note that on the surface of the gun in Foster's hand, no reflections of the environment, not even of Foster's hand hovering above it, can be seen. Yet the gold ring on his hand is just as reflective of the environment as the photos revealed. This, as the ring is on the wrong finger, as the photos exposed

Moving along swiftly as there is considerably more of Hillary's deliberate inaccuracies, others such as the Chinese Monks donating money to her and Bill's campaign with the help of Vice President Al Gore, however space and time press me to move forward.

Progressing, but not shifting course as we all are aware of Benghazi and Hillary's multiple lies, with regards to the events that night. Later Hillary Clinton came under increasing scrutiny for her story about facing sniper fire in Bosnia. The critical question is what exists, is whether she developed and engaged in a lifelong pattern of lying and deceit, it seems the only honest answer stands in the affirmative, by all means.

Pathetically we found this evidence even more than disgusting, this concerning the consulate in Benghazi. She, Hillary led us to believe the guards who took place were locals and were part of the Ansari al-Sharia and Al Qaeda groups operating in Benghazi. Furthermore, the source added while a handful of the local Libyans were the actual guards that the State Department under Hillary Clinton, were hired to protect the Consulate in Benghazi, on that fateful night with the murder of Four Heroic Men.

Whoever approved these contracts at the State Department hired Blue Mountain Group (a group based in Wales) and then allowed Blue Mountain Group to hire local Libyans who were not vetted, **John Tegan told Fox News**. One of those guards hired by Blue Mountain was the younger brother of the leader of Al Qaeda in Benghazi, again Fox News reported. Hillary Clinton is a coward and a traitor, who will allow Americans to die for her own greed and lust for power. *This is called* treason.

Again we find this is now being reported by Fox News in a shock revelation that Hillary Clinton, as Secretary of State, personally hired **al Qaeda terrorists** to protect U.S diplomats in Benghazi months prior to the attack that led to the death of those four brave Americans.

Vilest yet, standing over the caskets at the Dover Air Force base while these hero's bodies were proceeding a path towards their home. At that very moment she had the audacity, standing before the fallen men from the Benghazi Consulate, shamelessly lying to the families and deceitfully articulating a lie as to how the event was driven. This owing to that of a homemade video about some Muslim. In addition, saying he would be captured and dealt with appropriately.

These are the statements of a deranged individual, loathsome and despicable. It leaves one without the catalog of words to describe such a person. Then she places herself before the American people with the audacity to assume the role of Democrat Candidate for the Presidency, imagining she is entitled to be granted that position regardless of her treasonous behavior, this in spite of all the injurious behavior, despite fraudulent and corrupt activities, however she was simply again a liar and married to a coward who assumed her suppose entitlement.

It merely exposes Hillary embracing her obnoxious character, all the while manipulating the designs for herself as President of our Republic. If she hadn't been to the extreme degree, a person so cruel and vindictive, one could be willing to consider her sickness.

Hillary has used an illegal e-mail and server moving it twice to three private and hidden locations, this to cover her improper use of not only governments e-mails, rather official communications including thousands of emails that would retroactively be marked **classified** by the State Department**,** plus many marked Secret and top Secret. FBI Director James Comey stated, 52 e-mail chains have been determined by the owning agency to contain classified information at the time they were sent or received. Eight of those chains contained information that was Top Secret at the time they were sent; 36 chains contained Secret information at the time; and eight contained confidential information, which is the lowest level of classification. Separate from those, about 2,000 additional e-mails were "up-classified" to make them Confidential. The information in these had not been classified at the time the e-mails were sent, evidence shows that they were extremely careless in their handling of very sensitive, highly classified information.

We find her answer was to offer apologies and would refrain from doing so again, even so she has resumed her exploits. Enough of this evil woman and her endeavors. Nevertheless her Foundation remains under investigation and still she and Bill otherwise known as the Clinton crime family were sued under the government's RICCO RACKITEERING ACT regarding their foundation.

Let's take a look at the Clinton Foundation, remembering that none of the funds in the Foundation originated from their personal funds or monies of the Clinton's.

 An FBI investigation into the Clinton Foundation may, hopefully more than likely lead into an indictment, unless the Justice Department again interferes. This statement by two sources familiar with the probe of the Clinton Crime Family, telling the news media. The Clinton Foundation was formed by Bill Clinton as a political scam in 2001. Bill believed section **501c3** of the IRS 1984 code, U.S. Title 26 would cover his action. Nowhere within the subject 501c3
IRS code was I able to find where the Clinton Foundation qualifies as a religious group, or an exempt organization outside of the United States, plus collecting funds from foreign individuals, entities, and foreign governments. As for myself I am quite certain and of the belief it's no more than a slush fund for the Clinton crime family, thus they should be charged according to the laws concerning fraud and racketeering. The law concerning slush funds is money collected or spent for corrupt purposes as, illegal lobbying etc. or like style circumstances. *** Boehm v. The United States, C.C.A. Mo., 123 F. 2d 79i, 812***

 Nevertheless, expectantly the feds are actively and aggressively pursuing this case, Fox's Brit Hume said Wednesday, they reportedly have an 'avalanche' of evidence. A Wall Street Journal report says the FBI's pursuit of the case is rooted in recordings of a suspect in a different corruption case who spoke about the Clinton Foundation's alleged dirty dealings. The law enforcement agency has at least four other investigations open that involve the Clintons and in addition their close friends. "The FBI's probe into the foundation is much larger than had previously been reported", the network says. Some witnesses are being interviewed for a third time. Though there is much more, we will excuse ourselves at this time. Thus the Clinton Crime Family moves on and we shall see if treason is acceptable to the people of our Republic, as these two crime ridden individuals would indisputably destroy our Republic, for their own welfare and profit. I could go on, but for what purpose, my dedication and resolve concerning this corrupt woman, speaks for itself, I have trust in the discerning of American people for our Republic.

As for myself, this woman is without doubt the most vile, depraved and contemptable of any person, I could possibly believe existed in our Republic. I fail to think of another person so inclined, yet she had the vexing impudence and audacity to think of herself as president.

The Clinton Crime family now represented by Bill, had a meeting with Loretta Lynch on the tarmac as their planes meet almost at the same or very similarly time. It is understood they spoke of the grandchildren and of other mundane things.

This happen chance meeting had nothing to do with Hillary and her meeting and questions asked by FBI director James Comey at her home. I am sure if you or I were questionably involved with misuse of sensitive security and critical material, it's questionable if the FBI would come to our homes.

Nevertheless that's what happened, furthermore after charging her with negligence with secret material and improper handling of critical material, rather his inappropriate suggesting to Loretta Lynch not to indict her.

It is sad there seems no end to the corruption within our Republic today. Nevertheless, one could go on and on concerning this woman Hillary Clinton, though I believe I shown enough of her conceit, egotism and gross arrogance, plus evil immorality.

However as time elapsed we find Hillary is still attempting a path back into the limelight. Writing a book in which she blames any anyone person or group of persons, particular the Russians for her loss. When in fact she was a horrendous candidate and people were able to see her atrocious character.

One more thing prior to my moving on. As I am sure all know of the dreadful, brutal, mass shooting in Las Vegas Nevada. The evil Hillary R. Clinton stated, while in the early morning as dead bodies lay on the ground, "it is time we need to discuss gun control". While, at the time little, if any facts were known to anyone, only of a large crowd of human beings had been massacred or shot and wounded without cause. This woman is more than trash, she is vile and evil.

Analyzing the life of Donald Trump, it consumes many openings, with codas numerous, where does one begin to embark. In order to progress with the life of this man and the countless sordid details in his past business dealings, one must consider what he wished to achieve?
One issue that immediately stands out is the Trump University and the fraud this man perpetrated on thousands of young people. His promise of being capable for teaching them how to become just as rich and quickly as he. It was in itself a fraud on the face of it, the ideology and many details themselves were as such, illegal. I consider most of the methods were fabricated or based on illegal conceptions and his personal viewpoints, plus merely dreams by the students. Trump University: was a massive scam, so stated the National Review. What's more the university never was a university, as stated by the New York State Education Department.

They warned him he was in violation of law, operating without a NYSED license, nevertheless Trump ignored the warnings. Today after three major law suits, he renamed it "Trump Entrepreneur Initiative".

 The organization was never an *accredited university or college*. It never achieved nor conferred **college credits**, grant **degrees***,* or **grade**d *its students.* -In 2011, the company became the subject of an inquiry by the *New York Attorney General's* office for illegal business practices that resulted in a lawsuit filed several years ago, in 2013, which currently is a discredited and disbanded business, therefore a vanished enterprise.

However his nasty manifestation in words about the "Federal Judge Curial" (concerning the Trump University) being called a Mexican by Trump (which he is not) these words by Trump being a disparaging remark, created quite a stir in the substantially Mexican population of California.

Trump with his audacious personality and prosperous properties brought attention and countless players to Atlantic City, as he in addition to many others, sought to overtake Las Vegas as the country's gambling capital. Then again a close investigation of regulatory reviews plus the court records and security filings investigated by The New York Times. This leaves little doubt that Mr. Trump's casino business was a prolonged, stretched out business failure, but I believe it a deliberate action. Though we now pick up on his currently stated theme, that his casinos were overtaken by the same tidal wave that eventually slammed the seaside city's gambling industries. Rather in reality, his casinos were failing in Atlantic City and significantly so, before Atlantic City itself was protracted for failure and most certainly did.

 We find in his business transactions most were quite shady and in the extreme ruination for numerous small contractors. Though it became a battle for him as he could be liable in a number of states for false claims.

His claiming of poor workmanship in most cases would not stand as it was exposed as being otherwise.

Concerning business, this with regards towards America of 1990's, per the fix is in era, in particular for persons such as Mr. Trump. We need not question that people or entities roughly 150 small contractors, having laid tiles, marble and carpeting for Trump's Taj Mahal casino in Atlantic City, was of course a total loss for small business.

These were the men who work for people like The Donald, putting up their own money, with the naive expectation they will actually get paid for work performed. These are the people who lost everything they had, without taking a bank down with them unlike Mr. Trump. His excuse when asked regarding these issues, "their work was poor or else substandard" so I refused to pay them. If so then why should his claim of being "a great maker of decisions", would be believed?

The Donald Trump Corp., Bogus Bankers and their Legion of Lawyers don't really care about hardhats, iron workers and carpenters, etc. They are too busy reading "Trump: The Art of the Deal." Those individuals deal in devious words and promises, or perhaps smoke and mirrors. Rather they don't understand anything about the point of fact, or categorically hanging a mirror on a wall, any wall or keeping promises when you agree to pay someone for a job, or keeping your word once you state so. To them, life is one big Monopoly game, played with real money and with real people plus any individual's property. Anyone but theirs. When The Donald got into trouble because he owed them about $60 million in interest, they just offered him more money to pay the contractors, (insisted he use it to pay the bankers and junk-bond holders, rather than the pushovers who he duped into performing the needed or wanted work he desired.

Of course, for theoretical deals, truly a sweetheart honey coating style, Bogus Bankers insisted that Donald go on a diet in return for the $65 million bailout. He was limited to spending no more than $450,000 per month for food and clothing, but could spend additional millions to keep up his houses, private Boeing 727 and his 284-foot yacht Princess, which The Donald wants to sell because it's too small. Just paying for interest and upkeep on the Florida mansion Mar-A-Lago will cost approximately $2 million, plus equally on an annual basis, about twice the amount Trump owes Atlantic Plate Glass Co. but he refuses to disburse funds to them, just suggest if or when he may in fact compensate them is time squandered.

In general this is his mantra for life, his life, as he is of the opinion that not unlike Hillary, relies upon and presumes he is entitled. It is difficult to explain or attempt to rationalize his cruel, bombastic and crude attitude. Donald Trump is deprived of any realization of the average individual and any problems which they may have experience, though he feigns an understanding, it is all pretentious bloviating, intended to impress the citizens of our Republic, all lacking of merit.

Thus in my judgment both he and Hillary are despicable, self-serving characters, bent on using the presidency for their own advantageous endeavors. Of this I am convinced, neither of them have a decent or respectable past, both are liars, deceitful and corrupt persons. More to the point, are an unbelievable crumb of uselessness. I find myself amazed that from three hundred thirty million people in our great Republic, all that we find available were these two worthless leftover occupants thereof.

It is highly probable that we the people have shown little if any adverse interest and a mob like attitude toward the primaries on either of these political misfit phenomena. It was also a pessimistic mindset on most voters, I imagine so of both parties.

 Then we had a sworn socialist, one Bernie Sanders running as a Democratic, it would be nice if someone would explain, just how that would work. This is beyond my ability to comprehend as both of these candidates are socialist. Many people are possibly inclined to construe Sanders' calls for a revolution as just a rhetorical proclamation, I expect he's not joking about this, it's real and we should take it more seriously. His policies are rooted in a valid socialist structure and background rather than a liberal one. And despite what Republicans may articulate, there's no substantial dissimilarity between socialism and liberalism. Democrats and independents attracted to Sanders, need to basically think twice shrugging off his self-description of a more Democratic idea of socialism, the ideology of socialism only leads to communism, never the ideas of social democracy. While in itself is self-destructive as Plato, Socrates and Jefferson affirmed, it is simply mob rule.

 However, Hillary Clinton became the Democratic offer as candidate for president. As did Donald Trump submit his candidacy for the RNC. This is when all disorder began, persistent mayhem broke loose and was a part of both parties' narratives, inflicting lies, deceit all bound around fabricated issues, leaving the voters with little reliable information. Let us remember, it was the choice and the voice of the American population speaking to themselves. It seems the selection was ours from the beginning of this election for President and others offices. It was to an ineffective degree and long past time for reflecting upon past disasters, as a nation we are obliged to move forward, since we have chosen one of these despicable persons. Pray God will have compassion upon our Christian Republic.

A total of 17 candidates entered the Republican race starting March 23, 2015, when **Senator Ted Cruz** of **Texas** was the first to formally announce his candidacy. This was the largest presidential primary field for any political party in American history. On May 3, thus lacking any further chances of forcing a contested convention, Sen. Cruz the last persisting individual suspended his campaign and Trump was declared the presumptive nominee by the **Republican National Committee**. The Republican primary was a raucous affair, leading the disarray was the winner Donald Trump. An unanswered question, why did Cruz quit?

The Democratic primary was a battle between a true socialist Bernie Sanders and true to nothing other than herself, Hillary Clinton even though Bernie gave her campaign quite a surprise and disbelief, but not to worry. Old Hillary was up to her long standing of previous tricks. Bill pervert Clinton had a supposed happen chance meeting with Attorney General Lynch. This I stated prior and so upon target it ought to be brought to your attention again. An unintentional meeting at an identical time, in their own separate planes on the same tarmac, in an unintentional place. . There a discussion arose concerning their grandchildren and was of course paramonnt and a few other bits of chit chat was mingled. Of a natural progression was the path leading to any possibility of bringing charges against Hillary Clinton, of course not, rhetorically speaking, nevertheless no indictment.

Now arrived the battle of candidates. This with three debates of which each team decided their candidate won all three of them. However I'm of the conviction neither candidate gained a path forward on their intended goals, or citizens learning anything in addition concerning the candidates.

Donald Trump appeared just a wee bit more docile, while Hillary came off arrogant and generally stiff. As a matter of categorizing them, I've come to realize this was her, a methodically designed and structured life of lies. As was expected Mr. Trump was his rude, irrational self.

In the meantime Donald Trump slowly lessened his bombastic remarks to some extent, making himself appear a minute more presidential, rather than his vulgar character in the primaries. He seemed less revealingly brazen and shameless, while inflexible and impetuous concerning Hillary, so went the debates. Yet the people waited with anticipation, expecting to hear something revealing, why? When these are the same reckless, irrational and self-centered individuals the people had known and chosen, we keep electing the same category of deficient, unreliable individuals expecting different results, again *what fools we mortals be*. So went the campaign, forward march from each of the campaign teams. This till on Nov. 8th 2016 Donald Trump had received more than enough electoral votes thus becoming the President-elect. This result may have occurred since Hillary was such a poor candidate, and her team over confident.

Now the Hillary troops have one last very narrow trick, for die-hard Democrats holding out hope that they won't have to live through a Trump presidency, there was a last ditch effort, an incredibly long shot for them to latch on to a surprise twist in the Electoral College.

Though Hillary Clinton won the popular vote by about 3,000,000, all in California, while Trump had won an amount of 306 electoral votes, thus more than necessary to be elected president.
An Electoral College Voter from Texas says he's on track... to vote for Hillary. However this **Electoral College elector backs off a threat of voting for Clinton**. This idea for a change of an electoral vote seems ridiculous as the numbers above indicate those needed to (306-232) suggest Donald as President, since the spread is 74 votes, quite a challenge.

According to the Constitution, chosen electors of the Electoral College are the real people who will vote for president, when they meet on Dec. 19 in their respective State Capitols.

The idea of electors reversing their vote is rarely argued and was most recently bandied about after the incredibly close 2000 election in which George Bush narrowly beat Al Gore. And electors going "faithless" is exceedingly rare. Justifiably over 99 percent of electors all through American history have voted as pledged or promised.

Regardless, after all the hyperbole given the dissatisfaction with Trump among Republicans, a few faithless GOP electors could well go rogue next month. Even then, the new, Republican-controlled Congress meets Jan. 6 to approve the electoral-college vote, and would certainly vote to void any roguery, handing the victory firmly back to Trump.

The Founders created the Electoral College for two reasons in mind, first we are not a democracy and because they were "afraid of direct Democracy which is merely mob rule". In fact, Alexander Hamilton thought the electors would make sure "the office of President will never fall to the lot of any man who is not in an eminent degree, endowed with the prerequisite qualifications. I'm not so sure Hamilton's idea has met that great criteria, at best quite seldom since the ominous and nefarious Lincoln era.

However, we must move on as States United, our Republic for which all should stand as one nation under God, indivisible with liberty and justice for all. All the previous trash talk is not even allowed in football. Which brings us to the Pres.-elect Donald Trump and the ruinous attitude of President Obama. He truly assumed Hillary would win and has said "carry on his legacy" and the people should vote for her so his legacy would continue being supported. As usual it's all about him, our illustrious king, undaunted world leader. A megalomaniac, **narcissistic, who**

Sigmund Freud commented regarding the adult neurotic's sense. That it was a feeling of omnipotence and or, a signification of poor self-esteem. This thought ought to effect upon the individual as to reflect on the past eight years.

Whereas this issue is not about President Obama, I am obliged to speak to the central issue now at hand, Donald Trump Pres.-elect and Vice-pres.-elect Mike Pence.
It is my view and with the accumulation of data previously exhibited regarding these disgraceful candidates, triggered a feeling in the people to choose the least of the loathsome. Consequently, Donald Trump won a large portion of the electoral votes and became Pres.-elect along with the well selected Vice Pres.-elect Mike Pence. This with all the shenanigans which has been attempted by the Hillary Campaign, therefore plummeted into a cheap waste of trash.

A decision by the people as a matter of trust, a trust concerning government issues. Hillary's history and her demand of power, her necessity for the extreme, accounted for this craving of power, this while our national concerns were at stake. This issue of control to the extreme, to my judgement far outweighed any other elements.

While Donald Trump lies and deceit show no actions which were enacted or took part against our National interest. I credit the American people in their distinguishing the difference, in their lies and deceitful activities. Hillary's life was spent grasping for power in any form of government. This while Trump willingly applied his lies and corrupt business practices in the area of affluence and wealth. As a result the American voters, in my view, rallied to ascertain how Donald Trump's exploitations would affect them, individually and collectively. Likewise what effect would it have generated , having negative or positive effect would it have upon the nation. Furthermore, a good portion of the people were finished, plus sick and tired of Washington, with its assuming self-importance, to the point of failure to accomplish anything but hatred between RNC and the DNC.

I have accepted the call of the voters, decided through our republican form of government, Donald J. Trump with Mike R. Pence both men as chief officers and on January 20th 2017, they both were sworn by oath into their respective offices. Thus affirming to preserve and protect the Constitution of the United States of America. Now the true results lay in God's hands and I have faith His Spirit was made the real true judgement.

Chapter eleven

Donald Trump elected President of the United States

The battle for the candidacy of either party is more problematic than usual. Due to the large amount of candidates (17) in the Republican Party, and the bitter attitude of Hillary toward Bernie Sanders, as she assumed winning the entire election was a given.

Regardless Donald Trump was the winner, therefore turned out thus taking place as our next President, winning 306 electoral votes to 232 for crying Hillary Clinton. All at the hand of God through prayer.

As could have been expected the news media underplayed the attendance at the inauguration, "suggesting it was quite small" rather it was somewhat larger than stated.

Then moderator Chris Matthews of MSNBC's Hard Ball, *"Do the brains that got this guy elected president tonight apply to being a good president?" further said. "I leave it as an open question. I hope there's some connection. Otherwise we have a dingbat as president. It's hopeless, with terrible values and incompetence galore, and we're just into doomsday right now," he continued. "I'm just not ready to accept that sort of notion right now in my head. I have to think there's got to be a pony in this crap pile."*

The only reply to such a bizarre and crude statement, is to accept it as an act of desperation and recognize from whence it may have originated.

As a nation we ought to reject such ludicrous and offensively distasteful comments, coming from people who fail to accept their election loss. I am afraid this matter will only enflame and worsen as the Republic is vastly divided and numerous agitators of those who lost will continue their desire to spread critical and divisive ideology due to disbelief and hatred towards President Trump. The answer to all these problems remains as always, for Christians to gather, praying God will forgive and that all Americans may feel the need for repentance and forgiveness, thus seeking His blessing, His assistance to bring about a cure for our countless difficulties and tribulations.

Early in my well-intentioned and reliable statements, I submitted to you a need for a return to our God and Jesus Christ whom our Christian Founders and early leaders had their faith implanted. Consequently, as a result giving them the strength needed to carry on forward. Thus, regardless of the expanded time spread, today is no different, it's our same God ever the same, somewhat like our Constitution, though our Constitution remains almost unchanged, while God and His Son Jesus persists steadfastly.

Our Republic's citizens of which many seem to have forgotten the idea of families, the structure of family no longer seems to exist. It seems there is no accounting, we are without obedience to anyone or anything, especially God. We act as if homosexual life style is normal, as well the trans-gender person, both assuming to receive special treatment, why or how will our children judge or receive this conundrum. I find it a bit difficult for giving consideration of having anyone choosing which restroom or locker to use or enter. As if they have a choice in their determining their sex. How foolish these individuals exist whether homosexuals or trans-genders, why should they be entitled to any special treatment or laws in exception to all other persons? They seem to believe this is liberty, freedom, their freedom. Please let me explain freedom.

Freedom is liberty; *liberty on the positive side denotes the fullness of an individual existence, while liberty on its negitive side, denotes the necessary restraint on all, in order to promote the greatest possible amount of liberty for each individual. Freedom is*

exemption from extraneous control, from all restraints except such
as appropriately imposed, for and by the community. Those which
we are endowed with, the unalienable rights granted by God our
creator.

The idea that immunity is given to certain individuals from reasonable restrictions and regulations imposed in the interest of the community is ludicrous. As I have previously said, we as a society and government must backtrack to our heritage, where God was a real part of their daily input and trust, all else is pointless, childish chatter.

Another matter we have tolerated is abortion, a misguided idea dealt with in a pedestrian manner. While acting as if Planned-Parenthood could or would deal properly with this matter. The need for families, all must be headed by a man providing food, shelter, safety and leadership. The woman being a wife, providing wisdom, managing home needs and teaching the love of God, self-control and influence, yet discipline. Restraint of children's behavior is probably the most misunderstood but essentially the outstanding need pressing America today. This basic responsibility needs to be of men, as principal leaders with guidance by example.

This again is where the Christian church is essentially indispensable, as they need be neighboring the young, in every community throughout our country at every single level, yet seem asleep. I am persistent in the belief while the mega-church gathers members in numbers, it can't or doesn't normally reach the individual, especially the young. As it happens with our enormous national government in Washington D.C., it is both too large and far too distant from the challenges and questions, justifiably to identify or comprehend the situation, supplying too much **stuff,** then once more thus happening again excluding substance.

As I asserted concerning the mega-church, read Matthew 18, 20, "For where two or three are gathered together in my name, there I am in the midst of them". Furthermore read the proceeding verses 18, 19 of promise to the two or three gathered in His name. The need or should I say all are better served for small groups or small churches remains the same today as always. Within small groups etc. there is less division and dispute, thus personal issues become less of an issue and more is accomplished. Of course this my opinion, it is more important what's your opinion and strategy to employ, which pattern and procedure would you utilize, for reaching a mechanism teaching self-control and limitations on every part of our community and society.

Now comes the question how large is large, in most Christian churches there are Elders and Deacons or their equivalent, then committees and this is where I suggest one begins anew. These followed by more committees and committees to oversee the many committees, at this point I think it has gone far too far, for all of the above reasons, which has been continually employed by government with significant and obviously persistent failure.

Now that I have belittled and scorned our recent inaugurated President, whom I believe God had His hand enmeshed to a large portion thereof. I believe President Trump will receive a powerful resistance from the Democrats, this due to his willingness to move forward with his promised agenda. Let's remember his victory wasn't assumed, or was expected to happen. As Hillary was an easy win for them. Now the Democrats are in denial, they can't imagine or accept the results as true. I, as with many others may well be incorrect in their total assessment of President Trump, as it seems he may have grasped the overall enormity of the office. This as Democrats will never accept his presidency.

Nevertheless, the Republic is obligated to validate the transfer of power and step forward, as we will grow weak if we fail to support, respect and accept the furtherance of our national system for the elections of all public officials, as president as well as the persons of the congress. Issues are proceeding at such a pace, one faces quite a hurdle staying with them. Though I must comment on the President's choice for the Supreme Court, Judge Gorsuch, necessity demands and has proven this man being essential to the Supreme Court of our union of United States.

A 69 year old **President** Trump boldly told the American people the list of potential justices from which he would make his **choice**, and he kept that promise by nominating **Judge** Gorsuch." The best replacement for the past constitutionalist and academic intellectual the distinguished Justice Scalia, and so it came to pass.

House Minority Leader Nancy Pelosi launched a rather ugly attack on Judge Neil Gorsuch just moments after he was announced as Trump's nominee, calling him "very hostile appointment" and "well outside the mainstream of American legal thought.", "in fact if you breathe air, drink water, eat food, take medicine or in any other way interact with the courts, this is a very bad decision," Pelosi said during a CNN town hall gathering. As for myself, these are quite prodigious endorsements for Judge Gorsuch, and could not be more impressive, since coming from the mouth of the best liar since Pinocchio, remember (you must pass the law to be able to see what's in it) wow.

In other words, liberals believe Judge Gorsuch wants to starve our kids and poison our drinking water but otherwise he's a nice guy, plus he doesn't like puppies.

A prayer by Mr. Todd Starens, *Almighty and Most Merciful God, we beseech thee. Protect Judge Gorsuch from the liberal hate mob that is about to descendeth upon thy servant like a pack of rabid jackals. May they feast not upon thy servant's judicial carcass?*

Give our Brother the intestinal fortitude to resist the urge to whacketh the wicked as they are about to whacketh him. Amen

I am unable to improve upon Mr. Starens prayer and in many ways my only desire is for Christian citizens to get behind this God appointed man Judge Gorsuch.

Meanwhile today there are so many difficulties and struggles within the government of our union of states hath created and which the people of our Republic have established and are now facing. This is my desire that God will consider our weakness and have mercy upon us, as He already has giving us Donald Trump as President rather than Hillary Clinton, however, merely the lesser of two weak and corrupt persons. I consider it my responsibility to support his goals when they are in the best interest of our Republic. It is an obligation of all to pray for him, asking God to grant the wisdom to lead our nation with courage and Godly interest.

After less than a month in office President Trump has created quite a swirl of activity with his mingling of business practices and with a new approach to politics never seen before. A large debacle of his own making, was the execution of an order to detain a certain group of people from seven countries in the mid-east which are without a government able to secure their identity. However, it was how President Trump exercised his authority rather than his ability to do so, as shown below.

U.S. Code Title 8 Chapter 12 Subchapter II Part II 1182 (f)
Suspension of entry or imposition of restrictions by President
Whenever the President finds that the entry of any aliens or of any class of aliens into the United States would be detrimental to the interests of the United States, he may by proclamation, and for such period as he shall deem necessary, suspend class of the entry of all aliens or any aliens as immigrants or nonimmigrants, or impose on the entry of aliens any restrictions he may deem to be appropriate.

Then when an ambitious Federal Judge enforced a state of Washington law suit against the President thus stopping his actions, the President referred to him objectionably. Shortly after it was appealed to the Ninth Circuit court where it was sustained as customary, this court has a record of eighty percent of its decisions being overturned by the Supreme Court. Regardless the President has the authority to put into **position** such an action, perhaps he was merely approaching it by means of the wrong method, then again nothing at all was in error. We must stipulate that while he was hastened and was lacking an Attorney General for advice regarding this issue. Please remember this fact, which still remains the issue is the lack of a cabinet and is due to the Democratic congressmen acting quite deliberately slow has shown.

However, we still find ourselves in disbelief that such a woman would avail herself, actually presumptuously assume the candidacy for the Presidency of the United States, still whining and quite cantankerous. Nonetheless she is without any embarrassment, or to any extent an existence of disgrace. Is she actually competent enough to distinguish the feeling of shame or the degradation she has developed within herself, saying elections should be decided by popular vote, where Thomas Jefferson stated, "it would become a Democracy, nothing but mob rule".

This is a well experienced politician, spending her entire life involved in or around such endeavors. This with a blessing and support of a popular President after finishing two terms in office, how could she lose.

Then the most heard words, she was the wrong candidate, her against a loud mouth individual, who lied and cursed, belittling, calling her "Lying Hillary". Hillary was merely a bad candidate, not true and let me explain.

As Trump Jabbered "the election is fixed", problem is it wasn't, that Trump was incorrect and incorrect big. It was I do believe, he now understands why it happened, the people spoke in the majority of the states, grasping the delegates, though sometime thinly, but nevertheless gathering 306 delegates to 232. A large portion of the electoral votes coming from the heart of our Republic. People, real people who work to accomplish and develop the core elements driving the nation. Generally doing so on their own, built on self-reliance, thinking and hard work. The coasts, both East and West fail to understand the dynamics and ideas of the past and the influences of Godly people had upon their young Republic. Freedom to do whatever they desired, doing so without any help from government which was never imagined or expected. I do have confidence in the fact, that Hillary was a poor candidate.

One will find people not only in the rust belt, moreover the people in corn fields, wheat fields etc. all across the mid-section of our Republic. These are the lifeblood, the essential portion of what resourcefulness makes America and our Republic so ingenious are church bound, gun owning wonderful people. As a result, it's my view and when scrutinized one finds Democrats are willing to hinder President Trump, sacrificing the American people and their need for a small, but functioning union of the United States government. They simply cannot believe the facts, that their candidate clearly lost the White House, plus both houses of Congress, governors and state legislators, it was a massive loss and all are in complete denial of this fact. I suspect some of the Republican members of Congress are also in disbelief. An example, old Sen. John McCain and Sen. Lindsey Graham, appear as if engaging in disputes with their President is somehow a badge of honor, as if they're fighting for another cause and what cause would that have been in existence. This appears to me as merely the impression of excusing their failing bid for the presidency. This type of behavior on their behalf smacks of resentment, when at this time President Trump happened to be two weeks in office, plus he was without a cabinet.

However, upon further reflection I think the Democrats hate, really hate President Trump, so much is due to losing their opportunity to implement their agenda and his famous promise of **draining the swamp**. President Trump has found it more difficult than he expected, which to their astonishment, plus in spite of everything he is still in the process.

Now however the Democrats find it's impossible to move on any part of their intended goals, that of generating and establishing a socialist ideology for government. This idea could have existed and survived for them, if Hillary had only won the election. Perhaps Donald Trump was their most dangerous adversary, as he stood outside the norm of politics, which places his agenda over the Democrats, which for them is upsetting and maddening. Positive Republican enthusiasm in Congress and its drive remains quite lethargic. Please consider the call by the Democrats for an impeachment of President Trump, after less than a month in office. It appears his notion to drain the swamp, is an unwelcome idea regardless of whichever party is affected.

Think what the impeding forces do to we Christians in this battle for our faith, and freedom to freely exercise it openly with vigor. Again I find many so called Christians missing, I think lost somewhere in a constant stream of attacks. Then the following clergy with an impulse to accept government philosophies rather than Biblical facts, an attitude that the government will allow us certain privileges and concessions. "Allow us" What?
Are we crazy, are we not the leaders of this once great nation, how far will Christ allow these options to exist, when is the right time to move against these atheistic politicians ? There is no better time than today, as God will respect and support such an endeavor, hence ridding ourselves of such persons, returning to full enforcement of the First Amendment.

Again quoting Thomas Jefferson...*I tremble for my country, when I reflect that God is Just, that His justice cannot sleep forever.*

In spite of these drawbacks I must admit that President Trump has undertaken and achieved several beneficial measures along with some very sound cabinet appointments. The President's choice of General James Mattis, he being a very high-quality individual.

There are more than 22 orders, actions and memoranda he has signed thus far. I will name a few. First a very essential one, three orders establishing three tasks for the Department of Justice, **one** forces to fight drug cartels, reduce violent crime and reduce attacks against police. Then **two**, the orders restoring the Keystone XL pipeline plus the Dakota Access pipelines correspondingly signed **three** interrelated orders that would accelerate the environmental process. Further advance the smoldering infrastructure projects, related to the pipelines and directing the Commerce Department to simplify the manufacture permitting process. Gave the Commerce Department 180 days to maximize the use of only U.S. steel in the pipelines.

Again a notice that the U.S. will begin withdrawing from the Trans-Pacific Partnership trade deal. Trump called the order "a great thing for the American worker". Once more, an order that directs federal agencies to ease the regulatory burdens of Obama Care. Then orders agencies to "waive, defer, grant exemptions from, or delay the implementation of any provision or requirement" of Obama Care that imposed a fiscal burden on any State, plus "any cost, fee, tax, penalty, or regulatory burden on individuals, families, recipients of healthcare services, purchasers of health insurance, or makers of medical devices, products, or medications." The individual mandate is by far the most egregious portion of the Affordable Care Act and is exceptionally unconstitutional, merely a clear-cut fraud.

This is a partial list, nevertheless somewhat impressive achievements as many are promises he made during the campaign, which as a man who may be willing to attempt moving our Republic forward. I pray he continues his drive. I'm asking God to give him the wisdom to reject the strong negative attitude and turbulence from the Democratic Party and the many riotous and reckless socialist individuals.

We Christians need to pray asking God's forgiveness, granting the necessary courage and strength for our elected servants with support from those governed, while beseeching God for His support and assistance in all things. I truly believe this would bring our Republic back to the aspirations and basis which originally came about. Thus having the same objectives, a design for God inspired people, driving their United States government forward.

It is incumbent upon me to submit my reaction on President Trump's State of the Union Address to the Joint session of Congress, I think it was meant for and motivation in a new direction for the American people.

First I found he was quite Presidential in his demeanor, remarkably remained on his message with a strong yet calm presentation. He seemed to have seized the moment with aplomb, dwelt clearly on the issues, disregarded the chanting, hooting and hissing, exercising bad behavior and comportment by the Democratic Party. In fact President Trump was able to highlight his agenda, more emphatically asking them to join him for the good of the people. Further he stated, *"That the torch is now in our hands. And we will use it to light up the world. I am here tonight to deliver a message of unity and strength, and it is a message deeply delivered from my heart. A new chapter of American greatness is now beginning with a new national pride is sweeping across our nation. A new surge of optimism is placing impossible dreams firmly within our grasp. What we are witnessing today is the renewal of the American spirit".*

These words came across passionately, yet solid and compelling, one only wished the democrats had shown some willingness to bridge the gap, thus enhancing the future of our Republic. At this point in time they are in total disarray a shambles, their actions didn't facilitate his gesture.

The words continued flowing from him like a fresh reverberation flowing into one's ears: *"Then, in 2016, the earth shifted beneath our feet. The rebellion started as a quiet protest, spoken by families of all colors and creeds families who just wanted a fair shot for their children, and a fair hearing for their concerns. But then the quiet voices became a loud chorus, as thousands of citizens now spoke out together, from cities small and large, all across our country.*

Finally, the chorus became an earthquake and the people turned out by the tens of millions, and they were all united by one very simple, but crucial demand, that America must put its own citizens first ... because only then, can we truly Make America Great Again". He seemed to give the impression of a man on a mission, committed to a path where others feared to tread, doing as he promised. Draining the Swamp, great idea, we've financed and built one global project after another, but ignored the fates of our children in the inner cities of Chicago, Detroit, Baltimore and Boston so many other Democratic cities. We've defended the borders of other nations, while leaving our own borders wide open, for anyone to cross and for drugs to pour in at an unprecedented rate.

As in the past President Trump is fiery concerning the southern border, drugs, guns and criminals, terrorist crossing the border. This should be a deep concern for all, including the Democrats, I will finish with these words from our President. *"At the same time, my administration has answered the pleas of the American people for immigration enforcement and border security. By finally enforcing our immigration laws, we will raise wages, help the unemployed, save billions of dollars, and make our communities safer for everyone. We want all Americans to succeed, but that can't happen in an environment of lawless chaos. We must restore integrity and the rule of law to our borders"*. Therefore, President Trump first seeking the support of God, should move forward on all the issues he presented to the People of our Republic and again demands the prayers of Christians across our nation.

Now after all these prodigious words, the essential is the command of prosecution and the teeth for the employment of action, thus all those remarkable words could beautifully flourish. All coming from our past Republic and the God that led those profound men giving us this notable nation. President Trump has shown the willingness and intelligence, for bringing people into his cabinet which are talented and particularly qualified for the position of which they were chosen. It may appear presumptuous of me, but it could happen, because of God, we have a justifiably strong, though more than necessarily aggressive, but good intentioned, thin skinned bombastic President. However these characteristics in his temperament are somewhat more beneficial rather than adversely negative. Let us remember the words of Patrick Henry a true patriot and his proclamation on our Republic, *It cannot be emphasized too strongly or too often that this great nation was founded, not by religionists, but by Christians, not on religions, but on the gospel of Jesus Christ.* As I've asked before, is there none as he and other numerous superior persons, capable and so humble to serve, none to be found anywhere, somewhere within this large Republic of 320 million people. There must be a few, why can't we find a small stable class of genuine principled persons, I realize it's dumb-founding.

I am bound to be misunderstood on issues regarding candidates, irrespective the truth remains, and these are facts. Hillary will answer to God, if not the laws she trashed, I merely brought them forcefully and often to your attention. The same applies to President Donald Trump, though he has been given an opportunity to correct his actions and defensive attitude.

In no view point or position am I apologetic, as they are of the largest part facts, truths and reality, facts are inflexible rigid truths. It was never my attempt to distress or offend any readers. Simply to project the issues as they exist and how I found them. I am a simple old man, trying his beneficial best, with God's help, endeavoring to present our Christian Republic, from the past up to the present day.

Now is the time for action, making good on those beneficial words, in its place a congress which is not lethargic yet argumentative, seeing the need for moving ahead and not at a snail's pace. The Republicans currently have the advantage, time to grasp the opportunity. Please, you were elected by your own choice, that of being a servant of the American people and to our united Republic.

The office of the presidency has had a profound effect on other Presidents, somewhat worthy of same, others destitute of truth. At this point one is imparted with an impression, President Trump may be amply impressed with the magnitude of the office and its abundant responsibilities, struggling with his revengeful nature, thus we shall see before long, the results of his activities. Again we beseech a republican congress to act upon legislation, halt obstructionism amongest yourselves, which creates only boldness on the part of Democrats.

The time spent on Russia and President Trump is their objective, when Director of National Intelligence James Clapper and John Brennen CIA Director said they found no connection. Yet two committees are chasing this idea down a rat hole. Please we need to begin moving on, there is a considerable amount of work to be employed for our Republic's future. Therefore begin the work now as there is no better time.

At present the Susan Rice narrative is but a speck on the wall, everyone knows she is a liar, a pawn for Obama and cares nothing for our Republic. While the Benghazi incident first ran on five TV channels, Susan Rice lied five time leading the storyline, stating that the event took place due to an account, actually driven by one individual who made an anti-Muslims YouTube video that fueled the attack. Further adding that the assault on the consulate did not appear to be meticulously planned. Then when five Taliban prisoners were traded for the traitor Bergdahl, Ms. Rice called him a hero, serving his country with honor and distinction. Again she lied about the total removal of chemical weapons in Syria, now after denying her knowledge of anything regarding the unmasking of person or persons under surveillance, it turns out she was the individual responsible. So much for lying Susan!

Nevertheless, the real work for congress is the health care situation and taxes, both personal and business along with commerce and trade. However everyone notes congress has been unable to move forward on either of this promised programs. It certainly appears there is plenty of work, besides our congress is not an example of a group known for hard work, slow very slow as they plow along, as you know, we should think they would get it correct more often than not, even the odds are in their favor.

I do believe the missiles launched from Naval Destroyers was truly a great strategy, with small but some disarmament of the Syrian military, in a powerful way. Beautifully accomplished. It is important to know that they were receiving punishment for these barbaric events, after savagely attacking civilians. I am confident President Trump is undeniable positive with regards to this flawless raid. This displayed not only our military personnel and their equipment but our willingness to use same when necessary, as this prosecution has been long overdue in execution. Let's hope and pray he acquires a comparable program with North Korea, with the help of God and with little help from Congress.

However it remains on the shoulders of Christians and their leaders, as the prime examples for what it means being a staunch Christian and a true American citizen guiding our Republic. These are some of the most responsible persons to bring a fresh and much needed honest approach to guide our Republic through the truly dangerous path ahead.

Once again I speak to the actions of President Trump and his out of step, fast direct reasoning, perhaps on occasion overly fast. Thus this approach leaves the Democrats an opportunity, leaving another instance to show their hatred and excuse for the substantial loss in the past election. Thus it behooves Christians, in view of most cases to support him, as he needs a showing of support, sleeping or dead to the events is not a substitute for Christianity. As your actions are very essential for the liberty of our faith. This in and of Jesus Christ and liberty in general. Christians please wake up, your responsibilities are the ultimate among our citizens, act appropriately.

The congress is known for its' rules, regulations and protocols, I believe these action are too numerous and should be renovated and corrected judicially, rather to speed up necessary programs for our Republic. Again to bring needed and scheduled agendas for the growth required in our economy and to our people of our Republic.

Its appearance seems to be exclusive of any support from the Democrats, consequently the Republicans and their promises must go it alone, but keep their word. They had seven years to place together these plans for progress in the ideas. As for myself, seven years have vanished, nowhere to be found, while their described excuses still linger, never ending.

Those which are similar to the past and all the while they are approaching many deadlines of great importance. .

As a category four hurricane not seen on American shores in over a decade manifested itself upon Texas Friday night, also a surge of news came from Washington.

President Trump, in a period of four hours, officially placed a ban on transgender people, for serving in the military, pardoned a controversial sheriff accused of racial profiling. This man Eric Holder and was the same A.G. that sold guns to a Mexican Cartel, one of the gun was one used to kill a border patrol officer. Sheriff Joe Arpaio offense was stopping undocumented Mexican from crossing our borders.

The pronouncements were made in the evening hours while people many focused on Hurricane Harvey, which threatened catastrophic damage to areas along the Gulf Coast. This event gave a new meaning to Friday late night news strategy. This has long been a staple for Washington politicians looking to bury controversial decisions. As I read the voracious, predatory news media outlets, one could see the blood streaming from their gluttonous mouths.

There is only one group lower than our congress and that's the dishonest people spreading hate throughout our Republic, in general by long vegetated slanders and mendacious inaccuracies. One must research each and every word coming from their twisted, lying minds.

On this path of hate, it will only act as a groundbreaker, to which points toward great physical force. Sad, there are those who would rather go to war, than reach some ground for settlement.

We need to ask God's assistance and for His continued lingering support for things we have prayed. Those which we as a nation have asked many times in our past history. Praying He has the desire to continue having patience with His justice toward our Republic, may God's tolerance continue and to assist our Republic.

As Thomas Jefferson expressed and I am again uttering, "I tremble for my country when I reflect that **God** is **just**; that **his** justice cannot sleep forever". We need to pray for God's love rather than His wrath for the justice we warranted.

Again we pray for the people who have suffered and endured the horrendous hurricanes, Harvey in south Texas and Irma throughout the state of Florida. I hope and pray the clergy in all situations are praying and helpful to the needs of our people, as they know what God demands of them in these circumstances.

The issue of North Korea is still a very deep difficulty for all those who have to do with and responsible for its results and remains problematic for our Republic. May God once again step in and support us and pray for wise men to think.

I firmly believe we as a nation have arrived at this point, therefore God has given us over to those who wish to annihilate us, and extinguish our liberty and freedoms and our way of life. Please reason with this description of thinking, this ideology.

Since the beginning of my dissertation I presented you facts for your deep consideration and most final thoughts regarding our past and present Republic. Rather we must remember, *"we the people in order to form a more perfect union, to establish justice, insure domestic tranquility, secure the Blessing of liberty…must in union establish this constitution"*. …uphold this conception from the Constitution. Remember we are one Republic and may God will to bless our Republic once again.

After these times President Trump has quite a task with the Congress over his promises to the people. Saddest and yet a joy to see the President moving into action facing the obstacles ahead of him. There were four horrible situations, events to stagger any person with less strength, on Aug. 24 -29 2017 a hurricane, cat four racked the coast of Texas especially Huston and then the coast of Louisiana. This until Oct. 2 2017 of the massacre in Las Vegas by crazed killer, killing 59 and wounding 543 persons.

Meanwhile in between these wreckages was hurricane Irma, creating considerable damage to the state of Florida. Then another horrific cat. 5 strikes the Island of Puerto Rico, destroying most if not all their electrical grid, leaving the island powerless. There is greater devastation with only a sad description of their plight. Nevertheless the horror of their condition was added the chaotic predicament headed by corruption for many years. The governor of Puerto Rico has warned that it can't pay its $72 billion public debt, and says it is hoping to defer debt payments and negotiate with creditors, this debt due to a population of 3.6 million. The news, delivered on the eve of a private meeting with legislators on Monday, delivering another jolt to the recession-gripped U.S. territory as well as a world financial system already worrying over Greece's collapsing finances.

So much for the Puerto Rico's corrupt government and its despicable attitude toward the people.

The news, delivered on the eve of a private meeting with legislators on Monday, delivering another jolt to the recession-gripped U.S. territory as well as a world financial system already worrying over Greece's collapsing finances.

Gov. Alejandro Garcia Padilla is expected to air a pre-recorded televised address after meeting with legislators, who are still debating a $9.8 billion budget that calls for $674 million in cuts and sets aside $1.5 billion to help pay off the debt. The budget has to be approved by Tuesday.

Then 1:06AM BST 07 Oct 2010 The suspects face charges relating to possessing and distributing cocaine, and using firearms during a drug trafficking offence, the US Department of Justice (DOJ) said in a statement.

The arrests "are the result of Operation Guard Shack, the largest police corruption investigation in the history of the FBI," the statement read.

"Close to 750 FBI agents were flown in to Puerto Rico from across the country to assist in the arrests" early on Wednesday.

A total of 129 people including 60 Puerto Rican police officers, 16 municipal police, 12 prison officials, three Puerto Rico National Guard soldiers, and two US army officers, have been arrested.

In my opinion so much for Puerto, I firmly believe they figure a way to solve their own problems, rather than other. Not unlike the attitude we should care for them children.

Now I return to the diabolical prosecution of evil, touching so many thousands of mothers, fathers, brothers and sisters and so many others. I am at a loss for words… only God understands why this wretched event took place. On Oct third, our President coming from another disaster arrived to calm and console those people in Las Vegas Nevada who suffered so very immeasurably. In the span of less than 6 weeks, we as a nation faced four extreme disasters and our government directed by President Trump was there to aid, support and help in every manner.

As I write another hurricane Nate brings the need for additional help to facilitate the needs of those whos support is required, and have the assistance necessary to carry on, so promised our President Trump.

During the past five or six weeks our president has befallen quite a few monstrous disasters, it is my opinion he has allocated federal assistance quickly and efficiently. Furthermore, he waited each time till crews could arrive unimpeded by his arrival. Doing so brought criticism from those who wish to do him harm, he didn't care, waited too long.

Sad that our Republic is so divided, it not the President is always correct, rather he seems truly affected and concerned about our Republic and its people. Though very difficult, I remain optimistic he is able to drain the swamp.

I will close with this indisputable fact, John 11, 9-10 "Are there not twelve hours in the day? If any man walk in the day, he stumbleth not, because he seeth the light of this world. But if a man walk in the night, he stumbleth, because there is no light in him".

Reade's notes

www.ingramcontent.com/pod-product-compliance
Lightning Source LLC
Chambersburg PA
CBHW062135280526
45788CB00001B/177